May We Borrow Your Language?

PHILIP GOODEN writes both fiction and non-fiction. His non-fiction includes *Who's Whose?*; *Faux Pas?*, which won the English Speaking Union award for the best English Language book of 2006; *The Story of English*; and (as co-author with Peter Lewis) *Idiomantics* and *The Word at War*. His historical novels include the Nick Revill series, set in Elizabethan London, and a Victorian sequence. Philip was chairman of the Crime Writers' Association in 2007–8.

May We Borrow Your Language?

Philip Gooden

How English has stolen, snaffled, purloined, pilfered, appropriated and looted words from all four corners of the world

First published in the UK in 2016 by Head of Zeus Ltd
This paperback edition first published in 2017 by Head of Zeus Ltd

Copyright © Philip Gooden 2016

9 7 5 3 1 2 4 6 8

A catalogue record for this book is available from
the British Library.

ISBN (PB): 9781786694553
ISBN (E): 9781784977979

Typeset by Adrian McLaughlin

In memory of

FRANK MILES

(1920–2013)

CONTENTS

— Contents —

MAY WE BORROW YOUR LANGUAGE?

— Contents —

INTRODUCTION

'GOOD ARTISTS COPY; GREAT artists steal,' Picasso said, or is supposed to have said. English is a great language by any reckoning, and so it must also be reckoned as more of a thief than a copier. The title of this book is *May We Borrow Your Language?* and 'borrow' is sometimes a euphemism for 'steal', as the subtitle indicates. Yet to steal words from another language does not deprive that language of its own words; rather it is to share the original expressions more widely, in the process often giving them a different spelling, another shape and perhaps a meaning that has strayed some distance from the one in the source. English is adept at this. The language is a great borrower, a practised thief.

In the same way that many books are made out of other books, almost all the words in English have been made out of words from other languages. History and geography provide the explanation. Britain, sitting semi-detached at the end of Europe and slightly above a line drawn midway across the continent, was from the first to the eleventh centuries AD the beneficiary of influences coming from both the north and south. These 'influences' weren't exactly a matter of choice for the occupants of the British Isles. Rather they were invasions, whether Roman, Anglo-Saxon, Viking or Norman; yet each wave of newcomers, instead of withdrawing after a period of occupation, was to remain and turn into settlers and then, over generations, into citizens.

At the same time as one ethnic layer was added to another, so one linguistic stratum was laid down on top of the previous one. And, as the boundaries between different ethnicities will grow more vague if no constraints are imposed on them, so too did the division between the different tongues used in England – principally the division between Anglo-Saxon (Old English) and Norman French – became increasingly uncertain, when one linguistic tradition seeped into another. A little might have been lost or discarded in the process, but much more was retained and added when words and expressions from different corners of Europe found themselves living in close quarters. All this makes the history of English a complicated business but it also explains something of the richness and density of the language.

The point about constraint, or rather the lack of it, is important, too. Unlike other linguistic cultures – French springs to mind, for some reason – English has always been open to foreign influence throughout its long history, whether the words and the ways of using them were brought across by soldiers or scholars, by merchants or migrants. The great period of British imperial expansion and consolidation, which began in the age of Elizabeth I and lasted until not so very long before the beginning of the reign of Elizabeth II, also saw a tremendous influx of terms from around the world, whether from India and all points east, or the Americas or Australasia. In the twentieth century, the cultural and military dominance of the United States not only guaranteed the status of English across the globe but the slightly different forms of the language used in America as opposed to Britain have themselves contributed to the store of words on both sides of the Atlantic.

May We Borrow Your Language? is a story of origins. By explaining where a selection of our English words comes from, it hints at the range, exoticism and idiosyncrasies of our language. The arrangement is chronological, beginning with terms from the seventh and eighth centuries, and travelling through a landscape that is at first Celtic, then Anglo-Saxon, then Norman, and then increasingly globalized in scope. I have chosen the words partly in a spirit of **serendipity** (see entry for the origin of this word, page 203) and partly to give due weight to the contribution of each strand or stratum that makes up English as we use it today. The Anglo-Saxon or Old English one therefore outweighs the Viking or Norse one, while Celtic is inevitably reduced to some vestiges in place names and a few other topographical terms. Meanwhile Latin is everywhere in the period following the Conquest of 1066, not only because of the influence of that ancient language on the form of French spoken by the Normans but also because of its widespread use as the international language of scholarship and religious observance. And where there is Latin, Greek will not be far behind.

Sometimes, foreign languages have made a direct, untranslated contribution to English, and there is discussion in *May We Borrow Your Language?* of words like **pasta**, *schadenfreude* and **agitprop**, some of which seem to embody the culture that created them – or so we might like to think. Then there are a handful of expressions that, very unusually, can be attributed to a particular person (gas, **quark**, **meme**), one-off words that have come into existence by mistake (tranect, **mondegreen**), and others whose origins are completely obscure, sometimes quite usual terms such as **big**, as well as eponymous expressions created out of people's names (**Stalinist**, **Bowdlerize**) and portmanteau terms, slang and acronyms, and the occasional unclassifiable oddity like **24/7**.

This is not a methodical tread through the ages. The various centuries, from around the sixth or seventh to the twenty-first, are not evenly represented. Word creation goes in irregular waves, with a peak, for example, in the innovative and expansive Elizabethan and Jacobean periods. For contrast look at the difference between the first half of the twelfth century, for which fewer than 500 new words are cited in the *Oxford English Dictionary* (*OED*), and the almost 80,000 words cited in the first half of the seventeenth. Of course, many of these new dictionary words are offshoots of older ones as, for example, in the first recorded use of a noun in its verb form. But the general pattern is clear. Some eras and periods are worth more attention than others.

As a general note on featured words and phrases in *May We Borrow Your Language?*, words that are the subject of dedicated entries appear in bold (e.g. **lexicographer**); those that are distinctively foreign or antiquated English are italicized (e.g. *Weltschmerz* from German or *hyll* from Old English); and those that are familiar in English but whose origins or use are being highlighted generally appear in quote marks (e.g. 'android' and 'automaton' in the **robot** section).

The dating for first citations and the earlier forms of some words given in *May We Borrow Your Language?* mostly follow those given in the *Oxford English Dictionary*. This great work is indispensable to any writer on words and the English language. Its authoritative findings on the origins, changing shapes, multiple uses and sometimes contested histories of words are a continuing tribute not only to the high-minded Victorianism of its conception more than 150 years ago but also to a never-ending requirement to remain both comprehensive and contemporary. A dictionary's work is never done...

I'd like to thank Richard Milbank, at Head of Zeus, not only for commissioning this book in the first place but also for some happy and informative discussions along the way. Richard and I both went to King's College School, Wimbledon, though several years apart, and were lucky enough to fall under the influence of Frank Miles, the remarkable head of the English department to whom this book is dedicated. After his death in 2013, a post on Facebook – something which Frank would have dismissed in a few withering phrases – described him as 'in his time probably the most memorable, influential and successful teacher of English literature at any school in the United Kingdom'. It's hard to judge these things, but that feels right. A hint of why Frank was so idiosyncratic and influential a teacher may perhaps be gleaned from a story I tell in the article on **fuck** in this book (see page 74), an entry which is incidentally the longest in *May We Borrow Your Language?*

PHILIP GOODEN

April 2016

A NOTE

On the Principal Languages and Types of English
referred to in *May We Borrow Your Language?*

THESE ARE ARRANGED IN a rough historical chronology rather than according to the sequence they were introduced into, or had a marked effect on, English.

Celtic: the original languages spoken by the people who lived in Britain and Ireland before the arrival of the Angles, Saxons and other invader–settlers from northern Europe early in the fifth century AD and onwards. These ancient Celtic tongues included Cornish, Manx (in the Isle of Man), the varieties of Gaelic connected to Scotland and Ireland, and Welsh, as well as Breton (in the Brittany region of France). Even if they have survived, these have long been minority languages.

Greek: the language spoken by the inhabitants of Greece and more widely across the eastern Mediterranean. The classical form, or ancient Greek, as used for many centuries from around 800 BC was immensely influential on Latin, and then on intellectual and cultural life and languages throughout Europe for more than two millennia.

Latin: the language of the Romans and the Roman Empire. It was the language of government and authority in Britain during the period of Roman occupation and settlement, which lasted from the invasion ordered by the emperor Claudius in AD 43 until the final departure of the legions between AD 401 and 410. The main legacy of this period is in place names (as for example in Colchester, Worcester and Doncaster where the suffixes -chester/ -cester/-caster signify a Latin fort or military base or *castrum*). The great contribution of Latin comes later, both directly with the arrival of Christianity and then through the centuries-long and Europe-wide use of Latin (and Greek) as the *lingua franca* of scholars and churchmen. The linguistic treasure-house that has provided English and other tongues with so many words is sometimes divided into those words coming from the classical Latin era, roughly between the first century BC and the third century AD, and those from the later or post-classical period from the third to the sixth centuries AD. Latin is at the root of what are known as the Romance languages, which include French, Spanish and Italian.

Old English: sometimes referred to as Anglo-Saxon, the language brought by the Germanic invaders and settlers who succeeded the Romans. Many words deriving from Old English (OE) have lasted, with more or less alteration, until the present day. The dominant or official language after the Norman Conquest of 1066 was Norman French (see below) but it swiftly assimilated itself with Old English and the two tongues happily co-existed, to the benefit of each (see the entry **Pork** on page 33, for longer discussion and examples).

Norse: the Scandinavian language group, known as North Germanic in distinction to the West Germanic tongues, which include Old English, Dutch and Flemish. Old English and the various Norse tongues were cousins, even if not of the kissing variety. There was a significant overlap between them. (See under **Skin**, page 19, for words of Viking origin.)

Norman French: the form of French brought across by the Normans after the Conquest, and mutating into Anglo-French, until the tributaries of Old English and the language of the one-time conquerors merged to become...

Middle English: the general term for the language and dialects spoken and written in England from around 1150 until the end of the fifteenth century, and the precursor to modern English.

US English: not a distinct language, though you might think so to judge by the way it is sometimes discussed and vilified. The description indicates the minor ways in which English, as in mainstream American use, differs in vocabulary, spelling or overall style from the practice of British English. (See under **Fall**, page 88, for discussion and examples.)

WEALH

❧ (?c.690) ❧

THIS FIRST ENTRY IN *May We Borrow your Language?* is an indicator of the way language sometimes embodies truths about power and status. Seemingly, the earliest appearance of the Old English word **wealh** is in a code of laws issued towards the end of the seventh century by Ine, a king of Wessex, an Anglo-Saxon kingdom in southern Britain. **Wealh** signified a Celt, one of the original inhabitants of Romano-Britain before the arrival of the invader / settlers from across the North Sea at the beginning of the fifth century. Yet **wealh** didn't just mean 'Celt'; it also meant 'foreigner'. In its plural form of *wealas*, it is the basis of Wales and Welsh* because to the Anglo-Saxon incomers

---

* Rather poignantly, the Welsh word for England is *Lloegr*, among the suggested

the original Celtic inhabitants of Britain were 'foreigners', 'outsiders', people who were driven to the western edges of the island. Significantly, the word also appears in the second syllable of Cornwall, a region which for generations remained Celtic in both population and speech. From a linguistic point of view, **wealh** may derive ultimately from *Volcae*, a generic term used by the Germanic speakers of northwestern Europe for the Romance-language speakers of the southern part of the continent, and denoting cultures and peoples which were foreign.

An idea of the relationship between the two groups competing for space and power in Britain – the Anglo-Saxon and the Celtic – can be gained from the fact that, among its several other meanings, **wealh** defines a slave or serf. The word still survives, a vestige of old Britain, as part of place names like Walmer (literally 'pool of the Britons') in Kent or Walworth ('enclosure of the Britons') in Southwark and also near Darlington. Perhaps the oddest offshoot of all is the 'walnut', first noted in English around 1050 with the spelling 'walhhnutu', where the wal- prefix signifies that the nut isn't native but 'foreign', coming from warmer lands to the south like Gaul and Italy.

---

meanings for which is 'the lost land'. *Logres* was the word sometimes used in medieval writing to encompass the England of King Arthur, the legendary ruler of a pre-Saxon realm.

ÞING

VISITORS TO THE GERMAN city of Heidelberg who cross the River Neckar from the old town should enjoy a picturesque if steepish walk through woodland known as the Philosophers' Way (*Philosophenweg*), so called because it was a favourite promenade for academics and poets in the eighteenth and nineteenth centuries. From the top of the *Heiligenberg* ('Holy Mountain') there is a fine view of the university town and its famous castle on the other side of the river. Also near the top lies a man-made feature that would have been surprising to those same Enlightenment thinkers who once toiled up the *Philosophenweg*: a great amphitheatre scooped out of the sloping ground. It is lined with stone seats, now covered with grass and moss and a little eroded by time but still sufficient for thousands of people to sit or stand looking down on an arena that is backed by a raised, curving platform flanked by shallow stone steps. Slightly sinister and suggestive of an unholy cross between an ancient Greek theatre and an Aztec monument, this is the Heidelberg *Thingstätte* or 'assembly place'. It was completed in 1935 at the command of Joseph Goebbels, the Nazi propaganda minister, who wanted to cover the country with open-air theatres and rallying places in order to indoctrinate his fellow Germans in the right ways of thinking and feeling. Goebbels' plan did not materialize, or at least not in full. Out of the more than a thousand *Thingstätte* planned, fewer than fifty were constructed and the idea rapidly fell out of favour with the Nazi authorities.

While the Italians under Mussolini set about creating a version of the Roman *imperium* and produced only kitsch, the Nazis were after something darker and older, pagan rather than classical, an ideology that celebrated *Blut und Boden* ('blood and soil'), ethnicity and territory. Little could be older than the word 'thing' in its meaning of 'gathering' or 'assembly'. It is still in use: the *Alþingi* ('all-thing'; 'general assembly') is Iceland's parliament. But almost a millennium and a half before Goebbels tried to revive the idea, the Anglo-Saxons, also coming from northern Europe, employed the same word in the form of *þing*, with the runic letter *þ* or 'thorn' representing the 'th-'

4

sound.* Then, around the time of King Alfred (849–99), 'thing' took on several senses additional to 'assembly'; in fact a whole string of senses from 'cause' or 'legal matter' to a 'business', an 'act', an 'event', an 'item of property'. Plainly, 'thing' was a very useful and versatile term for it had acquired all these meanings well before the Norman Conquest of 1066. Early on too, 'thing' could apply to people as well as, well, things. 'This thing of darkness I acknowledge mine,' says Prospero of Caliban at the end of Shakespeare's *The Tempest.*† 'Oh! You Pretty Things', sang David Bowie nearly 400 years later. The word can go extraterrestrial. The 1951 film *The Thing from Another World* was remade in 1982 simply as *The Thing*, an appropriately vague title since the alien entity took on any (horrible) shape it pleased.

'Thing' is still something of a shape-shifter. Depending on context and intonation, it can be interpreted quite differently: 'It's one of her things' (a physical possession); 'It's one of her *things*' (anything from a private obsession to a

---

* The thorn or þ is found in written English until the fifteenth century. It was used in the first place because the Roman alphabet, adopted after the coming of Christianity to Britain, could not represent all the sounds in Old English. In particular, Latin has no 'th-' sound – hence the need for the thorn or þ. Later þ modified to a y-shape, one which is still to be found in the artificial context of names like Ye Olde Tea Shoppe and Ye Olde Inne. If reading these aloud, almost everybody would say 'ye' (as in 'God Rest Ye Merry, Gentlemen') but in fact 'ye', not being the old plural of 'you', should be pronounced 'the'. Somehow, I don't think accuracy is the main consideration here.

† Shakespeare uses 'thing' or 'things' a total of 835 times in his plays and poems.

mild interest); 'It's one of *her* things' (an area of responsibility which is specifically hers, so no need to interfere). Then there are the various linguistic developments and twists on the original term, from 'anything' to 'something' to 'nothing', and those expressions which are particularly useful for anyone struggling to remember or describe what can't quite be remembered or described: thingy, thingummy, thingummebob, each of these terms first noted in the eighteenth century, and the late-comer thingumajig (1824). Among other things, you can believe that life is just 'One Damn Thing After Another' or *ODTAA* (the title of a forgotten novel published in 1926 by the almost equally forgotten John Masefield), be reassured that 'it's just one of those things', or be exhorted to do the 'right thing' or 'your own thing' or to think on the 'last things' (death, judgement, hell and heaven in Catholic theology), be frightened by 'things that go bump in the night' or half tempted by the idea that 'one thing leads to another', or have 'a thing going with somebody', or simply 'have a thing about...' This centuries-old word is capable of new tricks: in British English 'The thing is...' is vying with the recently imported American phrase 'Here's the thing.'

CUMB

❧ (770) ❧

J UST TO THE WEST of the Oxfordshire town of Wantage, the village of Letcombe Regis sits on the edge of an area of downland that is a visibly ancient part of inhabited England. Nearby in the Vale of the White Horse is the oldest such hillside figure in the country, probably dating back to the Bronze Age, as well as a Neolithic burial site known as Wayland's Smithy. There have been human settlements here for thousands of years. Letcombe Regis itself is an old name and an old hamlet, one which is mentioned in the Domesday Book,* and so must

---

* William the Conqueror's Domesday Book was a statistical documentation of national property. It was a register not equalled in scope until the nineteenth century, and served less as a census than as a guide to prosperous landholders and their taxable status. The slightly puzzling name, which was only bestowed

predate the arrival of the Normans and the 1066 Conquest. But even without the documentary evidence provided by the Domesday Book, some idea of the history of Letcombe and many other places all over Britain can be inferred from the names given to those places. This isn't a matter of precise dating, except in so far as one can distinguish between 'old' and 'very old', but the often tangled and elusive history of place names does hint at the human presence over centuries, even millennia.

First of all it should be noted that the current spelling of Letcombe is not the one that would have appeared in the Norman records and registers. Earlier forms included, chronologically, Ledencumbe, Leddecumbe and Ledcombe before arriving at the current form of Letcombe in the sixteenth century. But if the name has changed step by step over the years, the basic components that make it what it is have not changed at all. If we split the Oxfordshire village name into its three separate parts of 'Let-', '-combe' and 'Regis', we begin to get an idea, if admittedly a very approximate one, of how far back it stretches.

Taking the 'Regis' bit first: this translates directly from Latin as 'of the king' and so 'royal', and shows that

---

about a century after its compilation, arose because it was considered as author-itative and final as Judgement Day.

the land was most likely at one time owned by the English crown.* The 'Let-' part of the village name, according to the *Oxford Dictionary of British Place Names*, means 'belonging to a man called Leoda', an Anglo-Saxon name. The -combe suffix is a common addition to English place names, one with deep roots. First appearing in written form in an Anglo-Saxon charter in AD 770, **cumb** is the forerunner of the later variants *coomb*, *combe* and *comb* and a term used to describe a hollow or small valley. Rather than a word brought across by the Saxons after the departure of the Romans at the start of the fifth century, **cumb** and its descendants appear to come from an older and indigenous Celtic word. This ancient term survives in the related *cwm*, the contemporary Welsh word for 'valley'. The -combe suffix also persists in plenty of place names, especially in the south of England and often near the coast (Salcombe, Woolacombe, Branscombe) where valleys running in from the sea are a common feature. In addition, Coombe/Combe frequently appears in capitalized form as part of a longer name. I spent most of my teenage years

---

*   In the case of a pre-existing town, the addition of 'Regis' indicates that it has been granted a royal charter, as Lyme Regis was by Edward I in 1284, or that it has received royal patronage, as Bognor Regis did after George V used the seaside resort to recuperate from illness in 1929. The practice continues. The Wiltshire hill-top town of Wootton Bassett became Royal Wootton Bassett in 2011 in acknowledgement of its role in the military funeral repatriations which passed in procession through the town. The bodies of service personnel killed in Iraq and Afghanistan were brought back to the nearby RAF Lyneham, now closed.

living on a Coombe Lane in outer London, and another student year on a Combe Road.

So the information which comes from the village name of Letcombe Regis is neither extensive nor certain, but there are tantalizing hints of the past, one layer behind another. There's a royal connection, even if it relates to nothing more than historical possession of the land. There is a link to an Anglo-Saxon by the name of Leoda. And there is certainly a *combe*, as testified by the current name of Letcombe Valley, through which flows a feature frequently found in *combes*, a stream (in this case a chalk stream known as Letcombe Brook). Putting these pieces in chronological order: the oldest part is *combe*, from a Celtic language spoken before the arrival of the Anglo-Saxons, i.e. before the fifth century AD; the next oldest part is *Let-* from an Anglo-Saxon name, Leoda; the final bit 'Regis' is added later to distinguish this particular area from a neighbouring village called Letcombe Bassett. This was originally all Leoda's land, but part of it subsequently came into the possession of the Bassett family sometime in the twelfth century. The part that stayed in the hands of the crown was Letcombe Regis.

There's another thing worth noting, this time about the name of Letcombe Valley. 'Valley' comes from an old French word, as does the synonymous 'vale' (modern French: *vallée*), both deriving ultimately from the

Latin *vallis*. This duplication of names, so that a place may in effect be called 'valley valley', is not unusual in Britain and reflects the fusion of the differing languages and terms used by people who have come to live there over the centuries. In Somerset, there is a woodland area called Vallis Vale, a Latin word and an old French word side by side, each describing the same topographical feature. The old Celtic *breg* signifies a hill (Old English: *hyll*), and appears in places such as Bredon Hill in Worcestershire and Brill Hill in Oxfordshire, so that the name essentially means 'hill hill'. Even such a familiar English street-name as Avenue Road is no more than the yoking-together of two words of very similar meaning, one French and the other Germanic in origin. Perhaps the best-known example of this double-naming occurs in the River Avon. There are several of these in England and Scotland, as well as ones in Australia and New Zealand. 'Avon' derives from a Celtic word for river, and the related word *afon* still signifies a river in modern Welsh, so the name really amounts to 'river river'.

Celtic has left only a tiny legacy to current English, but it punches above its weight because the survivals often relate to landscape features or place names like all the 'combe' words. The *tor* (meaning 'hill' or 'high rock') in Glastonbury Tor is Celtic, and it's significant that *tors* are commonly found in Cornwall and Devon, particularly on Dartmoor, because the area now covered by these two counties was, like Wales, something of a British/Celtic redoubt after the arrival of the Anglo-Saxons. 'Crag', for a steep rock, also seemingly comes from Celtic. The persistence of topographical expressions like *combe* and *tor* to refer to an up-and-down landscape can almost certainly be explained by the survival of Celtic speakers, the original Britons, in these areas after the Anglo-Saxon incursions and settlement.

CWEN

C WEN IS ONE OF several spellings of the word that
eventually became 'queen'. In Old English it originally had the meaning of 'noblewoman', 'wife of
an important man', usually restricted to poetry. The *Oxford
English Dictionary* cites a line from a verse version of Genesis: *Ða wearð unbliðe Abrahames cwen* ('Then Abraham's
wife grew angry'; *unbliðe/unblithe*: 'not glad', and therefore angry). But the word was predominantly used in the
Anglo-Saxon period in the way we use it now, to describe
both the wife or consort of a king, and for a woman who
rules in her own right as sovereign. When the Norman
French scribes got to work on the Germanic word, they
applied their own spelling and understanding of the 'cw-'
sound and changed it to 'qu-', hence 'queen', and other

earlier variants such as 'quyne', 'quene', etc. Old English didn't have a 'q', and the use of 'qu-' for 'cw-' was an inheritance from Latin. A similar process happened with 'quick' which was spelled with a 'cw-' in the pre-Norman period.

❧

BUTON

HERE IS AN EARLY version of the simple word 'but'.
It appears as **buton** in the most substantial and
famous poem to survive from the Anglo-Saxon
era, *Beowulf*, the story of the heroic life of the warrior
Beowulf. The only remaining manuscript of the poem
dates from the late tenth century, but its composition
could have occurred anything up to two or more centuries earlier. The relevant bit here describes the approach
of the monster Grendel to the mead hall where '*Sceotend
swæfon,/þa þæt hornreced healdan scoldon,/ealle buton
anum*' ('The warriors slept who should have guarded the
gabled hall – all but one'). The exception to the sleeping
soldiers is, of course, Beowulf. And **buton** is used to signify that exception, which is its root-sense in such earlier

forms as *be-utan* or *butan* or 'on the outside' or 'without'. This 'outside' sense lasted in Scotland where a 'but-and-ben' was a simple cottage consisting of two rooms, with the 'but' opening directly on to the outside, and the 'ben' being the inner room. Differently spelled versions of 'but' as conjunction or preposition persisted for centuries, from *bute* to *boute* to *bot*, before the word settled down into the form we have now.

The survival of the indispensable 'but' is instructive. Some words are so fundamental to communication and understanding that they will withstand the incursions of other, competing tongues. This was the case when the Normans brought their version of French over the Channel. Old English didn't merely survive, it provided the bedrock of the language that became modern English. It's been calculated that almost all of the hundred most frequently found words in English today, wherever it is used around the world, come from Old English. So the prepositions and conjunctions which English speakers use all the time (with, by, but, from, to, at, though, and, so, on) are to be found in Old English, even if in slightly different forms and spellings. Others in the top Anglo-Saxon 100 include 'a' and 'the', as well as pronouns (I, you, she) and the various forms of 'have' and 'be'.

LUST

❧ (888) ❧

L UST IS AN OLD ENGLISH word for a very old thing indeed, but it originally had the sense of 'pleasure' or 'delight', similar to the noun and verb *list*, now obsolete though surviving in 'listless' ('without pleasure', and therefore indifferent, languid). The 'sexual desire' definition of **lust** was first used in biblical or theological contexts and always disparagingly. Broadening out from its sexual application, **lust** was and still is equated with the pursuit of something non-sexual (money, power, fame, etc.), though the hint of condemnation remains. The adjectival and adverbial forms of lusty/lustily have a more varied history, with initial senses of 'cheerful' and 'delightfully' taking on sexual connotations, as well as ones conveying vigour and health, in which latter senses they still survive ('The choir sang lustily'). In an example of the way in which the same word can be adapted to different contexts, Geoffrey Chaucer uses 'lusty' in various senses in *The Canterbury Tales*, written towards the end of the fourteenth century: there's the pleasant one: '*Ful lusty was the weder* [weather] *and benigne*'; the vigorous one: '*And "Nowel"* crieth every lusty man*'; and the sexual one: '*As help me God, I was a lusty oon*' says the five-times-married Wife of Bath as she jogs on her way to the shrine of Thomas Becket in Canterbury.

If asked to name the seven deadly sins – assuming they know what the question means in the first place – most people jump straight to **lust** and will fairly easily recall three or four more of them before stumbling over the last couple. But this ancient list shows, in miniature, some of the sources that make English such a rich, well-stocked language. Avarice, gluttony, pride and envy derive from Old French words with Latin roots, while sloth and wrath originated in Old English. Each of the sins has synonyms or near synonyms which display the same wide parentage. Take 'wrath': there's anger (from Old Norse), ire (ultimately from Latin *ira*), along with rage, fury, pique, choler and displeasure (all from Old French), as well as dudgeon and tantrum (both of unknown or disputed origin).

---

* '*Nowel*', deriving from French, was a word to be shouted or sung to commemorate Christ's birth. In the more usual form of Noel, it became synonymous with Christmas, and from the Middle Ages was used as a name for children born or baptized on Christmas Day.

SKIN

W HAT DID THE VIKINGS ever do for us? Quite a bit, it turns out, at least linguistically. Among the many the words we owe to these marauders from northern Europe are some of the most common in the language. They include: **skin**, skull, skill, sky, skirt, egg, husband, sister, ill, leg, take, raise, club, anger, want, die, window, keel, dirt, they and their. The Viking legacy also survives in place names, particularly in the east and north of England, and as part of people's surnames (the Scandinavian -son suffix, as in Johnson, had a much higher frequency in the east of the country according to early records). To explain why and how these Scandinavian words were assimilated into English, when equivalent expressions for almost everything already existed in Old English, a bit of history is required.

The origins of the word 'Viking', now a generic term for the Norse seafarers who conducted raids across northern, western and central Europe from their homelands in present-day Sweden, Norway and Denmark, is something of a mystery. It's been traced back to the Norse *vik* ('creek or inlet') or to the Old English *wic* meaning 'camp', because of their practice of setting up temporary bases, as well as being linked to old Norse and Icelandic terms for piracy. To the Anglo-Saxons they were Danes, regardless of where they came from. They were also known as Norsemen (i.e. men from the North) and their language as Old Norse, the usual term applied today. Their incursions on the northern monastic communities of England began in the last decade of the eighth century, and before long those early pin-prick attacks became a full-scale assault on the northeast. Within little more than fifty years, half of the country was under Viking control. The rest might have fallen too but for the resistance and eventual victory of the forces led by King Alfred at the battle of Ethandune (present day Edington in Wiltshire) and the subsequent treaty of Wedmore in 878 AD, which ceded control of a large part of the east and north of England to rule under Danish law (the area was known as Danelaw). After that there was a lengthy period of co-existence between the two sides.

As with all invaders who turn into settlers, the Vikings brought their language with them. Like Old English, Old

Norse was a Germanic language in origin, and the two tongues had much in common even if it is unclear how far the two sides – Anglo-Saxon and Scandinavian – would have been able to understand each other, at least at first. In certain respects Norse was at a disadvantage: there was still a large proportion of native speakers in the territory known as the Danelaw and that, together with the fact that Old Norse was an oral rather a written culture, would have weakened its chances in the 'battle' with English. Even so, it left a considerable mark on English, more on account of the differences rather than the similarities with the native language. These have enriched English for the last millennium by providing terms which were new or alternatives to those already existing in Anglo-Saxon.

Take **skin**. This Scandinavian word applied to the removed skin of an animal, as did the equivalent Anglo-Saxon *hyd* ('hide'). By the early fourteenth century **skin** had taken on its modern sense of the 'external covering' of a person or animal, while 'hide' was reserved for animal pelts (though sometimes used humorously to refer to human skin). For the Anglo-Saxons the concept of 'skill' (Old Norse: *skil*) was expressed by *cræft* ('craft') while 'skull' (Old Norse: *skoltr*) required the more elaborate and typical Old English formulation of *brægnpanne* ('brain-pan'). The Norse *skyrta* was originally a shirt but the English pushed the garment down the body and turned it into a 'skirt'.

The Scandinavian *sky* once meant 'cloud' (the Anglo-Saxon equivalent was *wolcen*, later 'welkin'), and it would be several hundred years before it meant not just the clouds but everything up above us. The long-term co-existence of the two related languages is shown by the fact that many hundreds of years after the Viking settlement Shakespeare was using both 'sky' and 'welkin' as synonyms, though the rarer 'welkin' only appears once for every three appearances of 'sky' in his plays (sixteen references as against forty-eight). Incidentally, one of the markers of North Germanic languages like Old Norse, as opposed West Germanic ones like Old English, lies in the preponderance of 'sk-' sounds in the former, as in *skull*, *skill*, etc.

Three things happened when Old Norse met Anglo-Saxon. In some cases the Norse version of a word eventually pushed out the Old English one, as with 'sky' and 'welkin' or 'skull' and 'brain-pan'. In others, the words would be so similar that they would reinforce one another, rather like applying a second coat of paint. Anglo-Saxon already had a word to describe an area of low ground in *dæl* ('dale'), fairly close to Old Norse *dalr*; this similarity, combined with the hilly terrain of the north of England, accounts for the number of -dale names there, from Arkengarthdale to Wharfedale. The equivalent suffix in southwest England is the Celtic -comb(e) (see **Cumb,** page 7), although it tends to describe less dramatic features of the landscape.

Sometimes the differences resulted in completely different words as in skin/hide or skill/craft or sick/ill (Old English: *seoc*; Old Norse: *illr*); but there could also be an overlap, as in wish/want (Old English: *wyscan*; Old Norse: *vanta*) or rear/raise (Old English: *ræran*; Old Norse: *reisa*). All these duplications added to the general stock of words. Even where such pairs of words are virtually synonymous, they generally exhibit small but telling differences, as between 'rear' (for animals) and 'raise' (for children), for example. A more marked distinction is that between the Old English for 'to die' (*steorfan*) and the Old Norse equivalent (*deya*). Rather than abandon *steorfan*, English eventually turned it into 'starve', reserving *deya*/'die' for general purposes.

Another significant Norse contribution was to make clearer the distinctions between pronouns. In Old English 'they' was *hie*, not very different from the singular *he* ('he'), while *hiera* ('their') was similar to *hiere* ('her'). The modern 'they', 'their', etc. derive from original Scandinavian forms, even if it took a long time for the words to filter into standard English (Chaucer was still using *hem* for 'them' in the Middle Ages). It is also probable that the use of an -s ending in the third person singular (he talks, she runs) came from contact with Old Norse. It eventually replaced the Anglo-Saxon form *-eth*, even though this old ending lingered for several centuries until the Elizabethan age and beyond.

THORP

NOT SURPRISINGLY, THERE ARE many place names in the east and north of England that show the influence of Danish settlement and the Old Norse language. **Thorp(e)**, Old Norse for 'an outlying farmstead' or 'settlement' is frequently found, almost always as part of a longer title, as in Scunthorpe (meaning Skuma's place) or Cleethorpes or Burnham Thorpe, Nelson's East Anglian birthplace. Although Old English also had the word, in two slightly differing forms, there are virtually no 'thorps' to be found in the south or west, areas largely beyond Danish influence. (A rare example is Adlestrop in Gloucestershire, and both the title and subject of a fine and quintessentially English poem by Edward Thomas.) The Anglo-Saxon equivalent for **thorp** and meaning a 'settlement' is -stock or -stoke (Radstock in Somerset, Bishopstoke in Hampshire). A similar pattern of names concentrated in the North is evident with -thwaite (Old Norse: *thveit* meaning 'clearing' or 'reclaimed land') as a suffix (Bassenthwaite and Braithwaite in Cumbria). The simple *by* which is from Old Norse, and derives ultimately from *bua* ('to dwell') signifies a habitation and provides the suffix to many places, small and large, that would once have been part of the Danelaw. An area of a few square miles around Grimsby on the River Humber throws up more than a dozen, including Aylesby, Keelby, Grainsby, and even a double helping in Ashby-cum-Fenby.

PEDDER

❧ (1160s) ❧

PEDDER IS FIRST RECORDED as an English surname
(Will le Peddere) in the second half of the twelfth
century. Now it has the regional and Scottish sense
of 'pedlar', or a travelling seller of goods, which probably
derives from **pedder**, itself still an English surname. The
word is connected to 'pedestrian', in that they both have
roots in the Latin *pes* ('foot'), but the more immediate
source is probably *pedarius*, meaning 'relating to a foot'
but also denoting a Roman senator of lower rank (possibly
because such senators walked across the floor to stand by a
senior figure whom they supported).

Other English surnames which originate in words relating to selling include Chapman, which appears in Old
English (*ceapman*) and comes from the verb *ceapian* or

'bargain', 'trade', and Hawker,* another itinerant salesman and from an old Germanic term, as well as Tinker / Tinkler, found as trade names and surnames in the twelfth and thirteenth centuries and signifying someone who earned his living by travelling around mending pots and pans. Mercer appears early as a surname, but for a long time also retained its principal sense of a 'dealer in fabrics' and still survives in the name of the City of London's oldest livery company, the Worshipful Company of Mercers. The word comes ultimately from Latin *merx* or merchandize, which is at the root of such terms as market and mercantile. Other trades that emerged in the Middle Ages and at a fairly early point made the transition to surnames include: draper, dyer, chandler (for a seller of candles, then more generally a supplier of provisions, as in ship-chandler), cutler, cooper (barrel-maker) and tailor.

---

* Hawker survived well into the late twentieth century and probably beyond in the shape of snotty gatepost signs saying 'Tradesmen Only. No Hawkers or Circulars'. Another sense of 'hawk' – that is, to spit, and probably an echoic word deriving from the sound made by someone clearing their throat, first recorded towards the end of the sixteenth century – has no connection with the 'selling' sense; but that too was a prohibited activity for those old enough to recall the 'No Spitting' signs on buses and elsewhere.

WICKEDE

❧ (1275) ❧

WICKED APPEARS IN VARIOUS forms in the thirteenth and fourteenth centuries, of which *wickede* is the most familiar in appearance; other spellings include *wycked*, *wikcud* and *wikket*. The word almost certainly comes from the slightly earlier adjective *wicke/wikke* which in turn derives from Old English terms for 'wizard' (*wicca*) and 'witch' (*wicce*). Through the centuries some of the strength and colour has been bleached out of **wicked**, and the current use of the word rarely carries the sense of condemnation that it once did. As with other terms such as horrid/horrible, dreadful, terrible, awful,*

---

* 'Awful' originally meant 'inspiring dread' before acquiring the more positive sense of 'awe-inspiring' in the late Middle Ages. No longer used in this solemn sense, it can convey shock or outrage but tends to be used in a casually disparaging

etc. a lot depends on context or tone of voice. The slang use of **wicked** to mean 'excellent' or 'cool' goes back to the 1920s in the US although it doesn't appear in British English until the 1980s. It's an example of inversion, quite a common feature of slang in which a pejorative term is flipped to indicate enthusiastic approval; other examples include 'bad', 'evil' and 'naughty'. In standard use the first two still convey moral disapproval but 'naughty' long ago lost its edge. Once synonymous with 'evil', it was also associated with sexual behaviour and took on the sense of 'titillating', and so became applicable to anything which was tempting but forbidden. It was Salman Rushdie, in his days as an advertising copywriter, who invented the slogan 'Naughty but Nice' for cream cakes.

way. The best known catchphrase of Dick Emery, the now almost forgotten TV comedian of the 1960s and 1970s, was 'Ooh, you are awful, but I like you,' delivered by Emery in drag as the busty bottle-blonde Mandy, who would then clout the offending man with her handbag.

CEORL

≈ (c.1275) ≈

C EORL, OR *CHURL*, GOES right back to Old English where it means a 'man', often used in apposition to 'wife'. In Anglo-Saxon society it signified a person of the lowest rank,* but still someone with rights and possessions. After the Norman Conquest, the status of such individuals – the great mass of male workers – declined, and so the word too went on a downhill journey. In the thirteenth century *churl* denoted a peasant, a rustic or, simply, a fellow. Since rural life was equated with poverty and a general lack of sophistication and manners – at least from the perspective of the court or castle – the

---

* In broad terms, the upper rank in Anglo-Saxon society were *ealdormen*, the chief royal officers in the shires, with *thanes* ('ministers', 'servants') below them, and *ceorls* at the bottom. But there were gradations within these ranks.

expressions used to describe those who lived and worked in the country quickly acquired a negative tinge. The adjective 'churlish' (*ceorlisc*) had the purely descriptive meaning of 'relating to a churl' before the Conquest, but it later takes on its still-current senses of 'boorish', 'crude', 'surly'. One of the pilgrims in Chaucer's *The Canterbury Tales* is the Miller, '*a stout carl*' (*carl* is a variant on *ceorl*) who tells '*his cherlisch tale*', a story of true lust, farts and bottom-kissing which is crude even by today's standards.

Like the *churl*, the *villein* was once a feudal serf although at almost the same time the word seems to have been used with its modern pejorative sense of 'villain', or 'base-minded fellow', both meanings arising at the start of the fourteenth century. They share the idea of low birth, and the vestige of a linguistic link to agricultural work. There are plenty of country-related words which suggest, at best, ignorance and clumsiness: 'bumpkin' (probably from Dutch and first found in English in 1570 with the spelling 'Bunkin'), 'clown' (originally signifying a countryman and emerging around the same time as bumpkin), 'peasant' from French, and soon used disparagingly, and 'boor', a term related to the Dutch/South African *boer* ('countryman', 'farmer') and, like the other terms here, first cited in the mid-sixteenth century. Rather later are 'clodhopper' (1699) and 'yokel' (1819, and of unknown origin). Similarly, US English possesses a range of later terms from 'hick' (linguistically related to Richard/Dick) to 'rube' (variant of Reuben) to the self-explanatory 'hayseed' as well as 'backwoodsman', 'redneck' and 'hillbilly'.

PORK

❦ (c.1300) ❦

I N WALTER SCOTT'S MEDIEVAL novel *Ivanhoe* (1820), a swine-herd called Gurth and a jester going by the name of Wamba have a chat. They are speaking in Anglo-Saxon (or Old English) which Scott points out was 'universally spoken by the inferior classes', or the non-Norman inhabitants of England, and which he has translated for the benefit of the modern reader:

'Why, how call you those grunting brutes running about on their four legs?' demanded Wamba.

'Swine, fool, swine,' said the herd, 'every fool knows that.'

'And swine is good Saxon,' said the Jester; 'but how call you the sow when she is flayed, and drawn, and quartered, and hung up by the heels, like a traitor?'

'Pork,' answered the swine-herd.

'I am very glad every fool knows that too,' said Wamba, 'and pork, I think, is good Norman-French; and so when the brute lives, and is in the charge of a Saxon slave, she goes by her Saxon name; but becomes a Norman, and is called pork, when she is carried to the Castle-hall to feast among the nobles; what dost thou think of this, friend Gurth, ha?'

'It is but too true doctrine, friend Wamba, however it got into thy fool's pate.'

Having won the agreement of the swineherd, the jester presses his point home. It's not only the pig, he says, which gets translated into pork at the Norman table, but also the ox which turns into 'Beef, a fiery French gallant, when he arrives before the worshipful jaws that are destined to consume him' while 'Mynheer [Mr] Calf, too, becomes Monsieur de Veau in the like manner.'

Pork with the spelling *porc* is first cited by the *OED* in a medieval saint's life of Mary Magdalen, with a date around 1300. As Walter Scott's character says, the word does indeed come from French, and ultimately from the Latin *porcus*. The sources for 'pig', the still-to-be-eaten Saxon animal, are more obscure, but the word is close enough to older Dutch and German forms to suggest that it pitched up in England via a different and more northerly route from the Norman **pork**. Other pig-related words such as 'sow', 'swine' and 'hog' have definite origins in Old English or Anglo-Saxon. English is unusual among languages in having one set of terms for animals while they are being reared and another set when they are presented as food for the table. To the jester Wamba's list above could have been added mutton (French: *mouton*) as opposed to sheep* and lamb (both deriving from Old English), as well as venison[†] (from French) rather than deer (from Old English).

So how much truth is there in the assertion by Walter Scott's character that the difference in animal terminology between the raw beast in the field and the cooked meat on the table is ultimately a reflection of the difference between lowly Anglo-Saxon serfs and lordly Norman masters? A little truth, is the cautious answer. There's no question that the diet of the wealthy landowners would have been much more costly, varied and refined than that of the workers who toiled in their fields. They consumed the lion's share of what their workers raised, tended and slaughtered. But the dual terms for pig/pork, sheep/mutton and cow/beef are more a reflection of the extraordinarily

---

* The existence of a Ship Street in various English towns and cities such as Oxford (one of the places furthest from the sea) is nothing to do with boats but a probable indication that there was once a sheep-market in the vicinity. From 'sheep' to 'ship' is a short linguistic step or slip.

† Venison originally applied to the flesh of wild animals like deer, boar or rabbit that were hunted for their meat, as distinct from that of animals domesticated and reared on farms. Originating in French (and Latin) words for hunting, venison now applies exclusively to deer.

hybrid quality of the English language than they are of any class distinction.

When the Normans brought their brand of French with them after the Conquest of 1066, they did not eradicate the older language and dialects of England and Wales. Nor was their version of French altogether unfamiliar to the English, at least at the upper levels of society. French was spoken at the court of Edward the Confessor, whose mother was Norman and who had spent part of his early life in Normandy. Edward's successor Harold, defeated at Hastings and destined to be the last English-speaking king of England for almost three centuries, had spent some time at William's court as something between a guest and a captive. So the style and linguistic substance of Norman French life would not have been alien to the English kings and their entourages.

The two languages, Norman French and Old English, underwent a process which was neither a shotgun wedding nor a love match but something in between. Sometimes one word would supplant another. But, more often, words of similar meaning from the two languages would co-exist, or even be joined together. So we have 'law and order', 'ways and means', 'leaps and bounds', as well as sheep/mutton, calf/veal, etc. It is a historical and linguistic irony that the term 'beef', imported by the Normans and consumed by them in larger quantities than their Anglo-Saxon subjects, would one day be turned by the French into a mocking if faintly affectionate term for their neighbours across the Channel – *les rosbifs* ('the roast beefs') – on account of what was supposed to be the national dish in the days before chicken tikka masala.

ARRIVE

≈ (*c.*1300) ≈

EVEN THE SIMPLEST WORDS may have origins which contain a small surprise. There's an old French form of *ariver*, which is almost the same as the modern French *arriver* and the obvious source for the English **arrive**. But going back further to the Latin roots produces a combination of *ad* ('to') and *ripa* ('shore/riverbank'): in other words, to bring to the shore, to land. Indeed, in English, **arrive** once had a transitive form, i.e. it could take a direct object, as in a quotation from 1650, which describes how the wind coming from some directions 'may as soone overturne, as arrive the ship'. Although the earliest uses of the word are to do with reaching harbours, havens and dry land in general, **arrive** soon came to apply to reaching any destination, whether you got there by boat or not.

A trace of the 'getting-to-the-shore' origin survives in the idea that to **arrive** is to reach a fixed point, a definite destination, with an implication of safety. The word roots hint that travel, especially by sea, was once a perilous business.

The slightest tang of the sea also survives in another arrival word, 'accost'. Only used in modern English to signal a probably hostile approach ('I accosted the litter louts, and you should too.' *Daily Telegraph*), it originally had the more innocuous sense of 'draw near'. In its old French form of *acoster* it was used to describe a ship that was hugging the shore (modern French *côte:* 'coast'). But the word went downhill in English, soon suggesting an unwelcome encounter, perhaps with sexual overtones. This is how Shakespeare uses it in *Twelfth Night*. When the dimwit Sir Andrew Aguecheek is told to accost a chambermaid, he assumes that she's actually called Mistress Accost. Sir Toby Belch helpfully defines what he means: 'You mistake, knight; "accost" is front her, board her, woo her, assail her.' It's a coincidence that 'board' – a suggestive term rather than a directly crude one – should have the same sea/ship associations as accost.

HASARD

⤜ (c.1300) ⤛

H ASARD, LATER **HAZARD**, WAS a game of dice. This is the meaning and the spelling as it appears in a medieval poem called 'Havelock the Dane'. One of the pilgrims in Chaucer's *The Canterbury Tales*, written slightly later than 'Havelock' in the second half of the fourteenth century, is the hypocritical Pardoner. He is fervent in his attacks on dicing or *hasard* which he calls the '*verray mooder of lesynges*' ('very mother of lies'), and the word and its offshoots *hasardour* ('dicer') and *hasardrye* occur repeatedly in the story which the Pardoner tells.*

---

* *The Pardoner's Tale* (composed towards the end of the fourteenth century) tells the story of three drunken young good-for-nothings who go in search of Death during a time of plague, in order to kill him once and for all. Instead, they stumble across a cache of gold coins. As each plots to take the lion's share for himself,

By the sixteenth century **hazard** has taken on its modern sense of risk or jeopardy, while also retaining a trace of older notions of dicing and gambling. Shakespeare's characters from Henry V to Hamlet use the word frequently, and in *The Merchant of Venice* we see it in both of the related senses: of 'gamble', when Portia tells Bassanio, who is her preferred suitor but must still choose between three caskets, one of which contains her picture: 'I pray you, tarry: pause a day or two/Before you hazard; for, in choosing wrong,/I lose your company'; and of 'risk', in the message written on the casket of lead, which happens to be the correct choice: 'Who chooseth me must give and hazard all he hath.'

The word **hazard** comes from Old French and is likely to derive ultimately from Arabic. The *Oxford English Dictionary* refers to a twelfth-century history of the Crusades by the French archbishop William of Tyre, who imaginatively traced its etymology back to a castle in Palestine called *Hasart* or *Asart*, during a siege of which the game was invented. An alternative explanation has the word coming from the Arabic *az-zahr* or 'one of the die [dice]'.

---

they fall out and end up killing each other. They find Death, but not in the way they expected. The story of three companions destroyed by greed, which has folktale origins, is a favourite fictional trope, particularly in films like *The Treasure of the Sierra Madre, Shallow Grave* and *A Simple Plan.*

BIG

❧ (c.1300) ❧

I T IS CURIOUS THAT one of the most-used English words has no known source. Appearing from the early fourteenth century in the sense of 'strong', 'sturdy', **big** within the next hundred years took on the modern sense of 'large', 'bulky', 'extensive', although there is obviously some overlap between ideas of strength and size. This 'large ' sense is how Chaucer uses it, describing a character in *The Knight's Tale* as '*Ful byg he was of brawen and eek of bones.*' But Chaucer uses the word only once in the many thousands of lines which make up *The Canterbury Tales*, suggesting that the word was not as established in English then as it is now. The invaluable *Oxford English Dictionary* notes that **big** originally occurred mostly in the north of England and suggests a comparison with – but not necessarily a borrowing from – a Norwegian regional noun and adjective *bugge* and *bugga*, respectively a 'mighty man' and 'rich', 'powerful'. The only thing that can be said with much confidence is that there is a probable old Germanic root for this and for similar words in old Icelandic.

But whatever the obscure origins of **big**, the word has never looked back since the late Middle Ages. By contrast with what was for Chaucer literally a one-off use, Shakespeare employs the word, together with 'bigger' and 'biggest' and compounds such as 'big-bellied', more than fifty times in his plays. It appears in dozens of contemporary phrases and idioms. Cities alone provide the Big Apple (New York), the Big Easy (New Orleans) and the Big Smoke (London, and many other large places once known for their air pollution and/or industry). The connection between size, wealth and power remains in the frequent coupling of the word to nouns which indicate status, occasionally with a humorous twist: George Orwell's creation Big Brother, big cheese, big Daddy, big enchilada, big gun, big hitter, big white chief, big *kahuna* (Hawaiian term for a priest, sorcerer). Mr Big, the name of the villain in Ian Fleming's *Live and Let Die*, is an indicator of the fact that this style of bigness is a masculine preserve.

CHIVALRIE

≈ (*c.*1300) ≈

WE THINK OF **CHIVALRIE**, as it appears in one of its earliest spellings, as typifying the high-minded side of the Middle Ages. But the word at first denoted a group of horsemen ready for battle and, in an abstract sense, prowess in fighting and the fame resulting from it. The word can be traced back through French before arriving at the Latin *caballus*, somewhat ironically a slang term for a Roman cavalryman's horse, the equivalent of a 'nag' rather than a knightly steed. (The regular Latin word for horse was *equus*.) Yet this old nag has given us not just chivalry but, later on, cavalry and cavalier.

The knightly connotations of chivalry – honour, courtesy, modest behaviour, respect for women – appear a little later, and reach their fruition in the nineteenth century, long after the age of armour and jousting. It's no coincidence that in *Emma* (1816) Jane Austen gave the surname of Knightley to the most perfect and gentlemanly of all her heroes, or that Arthur Conan Doyle hoped to be remembered not for Sherlock Holmes but for tales of medieval derring-do like *The White Company* (1891). The 'knight' himself has unassuming linguistic origins. In Old English *cniht* meant no more than 'boy', then 'male servant' before it was promoted to indicate a man who owed military service to a king or other feudal lord. A knight might receive land in return for his services, so it is easy to see how his status could grow higher still.

Another significant concept brought from France is *curteisye*, a combination of gracefulness and politeness. The adjective *curtois* ('courteous') emerged towards the end of the thirteenth century to describe the well-mannered behaviour expected in a king or prince's court (Middle English *curt*: 'court'). Later on, 'courtesy' dropped a few letters to provide us with 'curtsy' or the deferential bending of the knee or little bobbing motion in front of a person of higher rank. Less respectably, 'court' is also at the root of 'courtesan', a court-mistress or high-class prostitute. Another key word in English literary and cultural history, *gentilesse* (1340) is closely related to honour, chivalry and courtesy. Signifying gentleness of birth (i.e. from a noble or upper-class family), *gentilesse* then spread to encompass the code which ought to govern the behaviour of people from that kind of background. For women it implied refinement, delicacy, sympathy. For men, honour and honesty in deeds and words. Then the notion expanded to cover other classes besides the courtly one. A middle-class writer like Geoffrey Chaucer – the son of a London wine-importer even if he was attached to a royal household as a young man and even if his sister-in-law, Katherine Swynford, was the long-term mistress and then wife of John of Gaunt – was concerned to show that you didn't have to be well born to possess *gentilesse*. It was a state of mind and a correct way of feeling and responding rather than a matter of blood and breeding. Although it is a distantly related idea, *gentilesse* is not the same as the modern 'gentleness'. The medieval concept survives in 'gentleman' and the now archaic 'gentlewoman' as well as in 'genteel', formerly a term of approval but now pejorative because a genteel person is copying the manners of someone higher up the social scale but in a superficial or unconvincing way.

VICAR

～ (EARLY FOURTEENTH CENTURY) ～

THE POPE IS DESCRIBED as 'God's vicar' in a medieval poem of 1340, but it wasn't necessarily a gender-specific word at the time, since Geoffrey Chaucer – in a poem that was written at a slightly later date – tells how God made the Virgin Mary into the '*vicaire and maistresse/Of al this world*'. **Vicar** comes, via French, from the Latin *vicarius* or substitute. The Latin original survives more directly in modern English in 'vicarious' to describe a second-hand or transferred experience ('I enjoy vicarious pleasure through helping friends select gifts for their mums.' *Guardian*), and in the related prefix *vice* ('in place of', derived from Latin), as in a vice-president or a viceroy, the governor who ruled as representative of a king or queen. The English **vicar**, once again as unisex a term as it was in

Chaucer's time, derived not so much from the idea that the priest was standing in for/representing God on earth but from the fact that he was acting in place of the more senior parson or rector, who would have been entitled, as the incumbent, to receive the tithes from the parish. From the early fifteenth century the 'vicarage' has described the vicar's benefice (i.e. the area or parish for which he is responsible and which provides his living), and from about a century later the word extends to cover his residence.

Whatever the English think about the **vicar**, they love the 'vicarage', a state of mind as much as a place, one where anything is possible from a tea party to a murder. Rupert Brooke's homesick 'The Old Vicarage, Granchester', written in Berlin in 1912, ends with the famous lines 'Stands the Church clock at ten to three?/And is there honey still for tea?' The title of Agatha Christie's *The Murder at the Vicarage* (1930), the first of her mysteries to feature Miss Marple, was perhaps meant to shock or intrigue by coupling a dastardly crime with a priestly residence. Strangely, it served only to reinforce the cosy, domestic nature of the place. And the supposedly sedate and genteel quality of a 'vicarage tea party' has long been used as a standard by which to judge things that are far from sedate or genteel. The usual media formula is that if you thought X was bad, shocking, disturbing, then you should really take a glance at the much worse Y because it makes X look like a 'vicarage tea party'.

LAVATORY

⪍ (1370S / EARLY TWENTIETH CENTURY) ⪎

T HIS WORD HAS GONE round in a circle, beginning in the Middle Ages with one meaning
before acquiring several related senses in the
next centuries and finally coming back to rest in its modern guise as… as, well, what should it be called? We'll
come to that later. First the word itself. Deriving originally from Latin, **lavatory** denoted a basin, somewhere to
wash one's hands or feet, as in the contemporary French
equivalent *lavabo*. Later, it would apply also to the act of
washing, especially in a ritual and religious sense. Around
the middle of the nineteenth century it becomes the word
for a room containing the wherewithal to wash oneself.
And when such rooms began to be equipped with a water-
closet, **lavatory** grew to encompass that item as well.

Since a **lavatory** is a kind of basin, or water-filled pan, the word might be said to have returned to its original medieval sense, though not the medieval function of hand-washing.

The problem of what to call the **lavatory** forms an interesting study in itself, one that is more social than linguistic. Certainly there's no shortage of twenty-first-century synonyms for the thing. On the genteel side are terms like these: bathroom, washroom, restroom, the smallest room in the house, the little boys'/girls' room, powder room, comfort station, ladies, gentlemen/gents, conveniences, and even the rather old-fashioned 'offices'. Next on the lavatorial spectrum is a clutch of functionally descriptive terms such as water-closet (w.c.), toilet, urinal, latrine, commode. But it's in the murky world of slang that the alternative terms for the **lavatory** really thrive: loo, lav, lavvy, can, bog, john (US), jakes, cottage, thunderbox,* shitter/shithouse,

---

* These three slang expressions deserve a footnote. 'Jakes' is old – Shakespeare has it in an insult in *King Lear* ('I will tread this unbolted villain into mortar and daub the wall of a jakes with him') – but the origin is uncertain. It may come from the name Jacques or some variant of it, and Shakespeare again puns on jakes in the lavatorial sense in the character of Jacques in *As You Like It*. In this respect it's interesting to note the US slang term 'john'. The thunderbox, which seems to have British military associations and which features prominently in *Men at Arms* (1952), the first of Evelyn Waugh's trilogy about the Second World War, was a portable commode enclosed in a wooden box. The reverberating effect caused by the wooden enclosure when the box is in operation no doubt explains the thunder part of the word. 'Cottage' is gay argot for a pick-up or sex in a public lavatory, first used as a verb in the early 1970s but appearing as a noun before then. The homely style and cute dimensions of some of London's older public

crapper, karzy (probably from Italian *casa*: 'house') and throne room, as well as regional terms like 'netty' (in northeast England), 'cludgie' (Scottish, mainly Glasgow) or the specialist 'heads' (nautical slang), to which one could add several expressions for the chamberpot (potty, po, jordan, jerry, piss pot).

That there are so many terms for **lavatory** is a signal that what goes on there – urinating and defecating, or pissing and shitting – is on the edge of being a taboo subject, or at least something which is not to be talked about in polite society. That's why expressions such as 'spend a penny' or 'make a comfort stop' or 'bathroom break' came into existence, as well as what is perhaps the ultimate euphemistic question to be asked of visitors just arriving at your home: 'Would you like to wash your hands?' At the same time, and in common with other taboo subjects, the **lavatory** and its function in disposing of human waste in a hygienic, secluded fashion is a source of a deep yet uneasy fascination. Toilet humour – or, more formally, scatological jokes – is a favourite with children but, in a guilty kind of way, most adults aren't averse to it either.

The word 'toilet' has gone through a similar transformation. Deriving from French terms to do with cloth (*toile*,

---

lavatories, such as the one in Pond Square, Highgate, made 'cottage' an almost inevitable term.

toilette), it extended itself to cover, literally so, the dressing-table on which the cloth might be spread. Then it applies to all the items required for dressing, doing the hair, the cosmetics on the dressing-table. Right up to the early twentieth century, doing/making one's toilet – sometimes toilette – meant getting ready for the day. Slightly earlier, and in America, toilet comes to be used in the sense of public conveniences and then to mean a w.c. or **lavatory**. This definition has now driven out the earlier ones. It is a word which has come down in the world from its elegant beginnings. You could say that the toilette has gone down the toilet.

Talking of toilet humour: a regular film gag involves some hick up from the sticks and, whether in the big city or on a first trip abroad, mistaking a bidet for a **lavatory**. Here, and quite by accident, the old and the new senses of **lavatory** coincide, since sophisticated continentals use the bidet as a basin for washing in while ignorant Brits and Ozzies assume it has an excremental purpose. The gag crops up in *Crocodile Dundee* (1986) and *The Inbetweeners* (2011), where after some bafflement a hotel bidet is said to be, respectively, a place to clean your shoes and a kid's toilet. The word 'bidet' actually derives from a French term for a pony, something which can be ridden, and so came to apply to a kind of low tub which can also be ridden or straddled.

SALARY

❧ (1377) ❧

S ALARY, WITH THE SPELLING *salarye*, is first found in Middle English in the allegorical poem *Piers Plowman*, but the shape and sense of the word was provided much earlier by the Latin word for salt, *sal*. In the first century AD the Roman historian Pliny wrote that Roman soldiers were at one time paid in salt, thus giving rise to the word *salarium*. It's more likely that the soldiers were given an allowance which could be used for buying salt and, presumably, other things as well, but the link with pay is a reminder of times when salt was a valuable commodity, used not only to add flavour but as a preservative. The application of **salary** was generally restricted in the fifteenth century to the stipend paid to priests but thereafter it takes on its modern sense of regular payment made for regular work, usually of the non-manual sort. It has produced a couple of twentieth-century offshoots such as *salariat* denoting salary-earners collectively (along the lines of proletariat, commentariat, etc.) and the curious Japanese term 'salaryman' to characterize a male white-collar employee. Given the changing nature of work and employment, such terms look increasingly obsolete.

The distinction between the **salary**, paid at monthly or longer intervals, and 'wages', paid daily or weekly and usually for manual or other non-professional work, does not seem to have been very marked in English in the Middle Ages. Deriving ultimately from a Germanic word meaning 'pledge' or 'security' and appearing in the monetary sense in both singular (first cited 1338) and plural (1377) forms, 'wage'(s) is a more versatile term than **salary**. It lends itself more readily to metaphor ('wages of sin' or the film title *Wages of Fear* – in the French original *Le salaire de la peur*) and is part of several compound expressions such as 'living wage', 'wage slip', 'wage packet', 'wage restraint', 'wage-slave', all of which indicate what was historically the case: that the mass of working people were 'wage' earners, to be paid daily or weekly and regarded as skilled or unskilled, as opposed to the professional, salaried class.

There are only a handful of terms synonymous with **salary** and wages, that is, ones describing a regular rather than a one-off payment. 'Earning'(s) in the sense of

'recompense' or 'reward' is found in Old English in different spellings, but only acquired its 'money got through
work' meaning in the sixteenth century. 'Income' at first
meant exactly what the constituent parts of the word suggest, a 'coming in' or 'arrival', then 'entrance-fee' and finally
'money received', although not necessarily through working for it, as the expression 'private income' still indicates.
Given the importance of earning a living, it's surprising that, although there are many slang terms for money,
there are very few for 'wages'. One is 'screw', dating from
the mid-Victorian period and of uncertain origin, though
Jonathon Green speculates in his *Dictionary of Slang* that it
derived from what the worker might 'screw' out of a tight-
fisted employer.

A similar distinction to that between the salaried
worker and the wage-earner, one which is as much to
do with status and class as it is to do with the amount of
money earned, emerges when looking at the various terms
for smaller, one-off payments. The professional classes
have 'fees' (originally from French) and 'emoluments'
(Latin), while the workers, particularly those who wait on
others, earn 'tips' (slang, perhaps connected to the idea
of a light touch as money is passed over) and 'gratuities'
(French/Latin). Two French terms are worth glancing at,
since they occupy opposite ends of the spectrum. A *pour-
boire* is a tip, but the use of French draws a veil over its

literal meaning of 'for drinking'. English once had a similar expression in 'drink-money'. The other is *douceur*, French for 'sweetness', and sometimes found in the expression *douceur de vivre* ('sweetness of life') but also used occasionally in English for a gift, usually monetary, which is intended to soften up the recipient. In other and harsher words: a bribe, bung or back-hander.

TRAGEDY

≈ (c.1380) ≈

T HE FINANCIAL TROUBLES THAT have assailed Greece for several years have inevitably prompted newspaper subeditors to come up with headlines like 'Greece's economic crisis goes on, like an odyssey without end' (*Guardian*, January 2016). Expressions such as 'trauma', 'tragedy', 'crisis' and 'catastrophe' are not only routine but also appropriate, since each of these terms derives from ancient Greek. 'Trauma' originally signified a wound while 'crisis' meant decision and 'catastrophe' a sudden turn. So far, so straightforward, even if it's interesting to observe that catastrophe didn't initially mean the same as disaster but something closer to 'outcome' or 'denouement'. But **tragedy** has an odder history. It seems to be a combination of two words: *tragos*, which translates as 'goat', and *ode* ('song'). So goat-song. One explanation is that the prize in Athenian play competitions was a live goat, which if nothing else puts a different spin on the expression 'to get one's goat'. The unfortunate animal might even be sacrificed to the accompaniment of a sung lament. Hence the goat-song became bound up with Greek drama.

Towards the end of the fourteenth century, when **tragedy** first appears in the English language, it characterizes a poem dealing with a grand but sorrowful event. Such a work usually involved kings, princes, generals; it always ended in downfall and death. Sending out *Troilus & Criseyde** into the world, Geoffrey Chaucer said of his tale of the star-crossed lovers of Troy: '*Go litel bok, go litel myn Tregedie.*' The 'little' bit is ironic as the poem is thousands of lines long, but the 'tragedy' part is accurate enough, since Troilus is a prince who dies in battle after being betrayed by Criseyde. Two hundred years later Shakespeare produced his own version of the story in *Troilus and Cressida*, and more famous tragedies such as *Hamlet*, *King Lear* and *Othello* also fit the template of a great

---

* In the same poem, probably completed in the mid-1380s, Chaucer also introduced 'pander' into English or rather the character from which that word derives. Pandarus is the uncle to Criseyde and encourages the liaison between his niece and Troilus in a slightly creepy way. He's a go-between for the lovers, and so plays the part of pimp or procurer – or pander. The verb sense of pander, meaning to 'gratify', to 'indulge another's tastes or whims', comes later.

figure brought down through a combination of fate, circumstances and some error or failing of his own. The word soon escaped its literary and poetic confines to be applied to any event that causes destruction and death, probably widespread but without necessarily involving the downfall of a great and noble individual. **Tragedy** still retains something of its force, though the word has been watered down so that missing a goal or mislaying a (winning) lottery ticket could be described as tragic.

Several other terms associated with classical Greek drama have also entered the language. The 'protagonist' was the principal character in a dramatic work. Such a figure will probably endure a moment of dramatic 'anagnorisis', which is a sudden recognition or self-discovery. However obscure the word may sound, the moment is a very familiar one in drama. It occurs at the end of Shakespeare's *Twelfth Night* when the twin brother and sister, Sebastian and Viola, who have been separated after a shipwreck and believe each other dead, are reunited. The discovery aspect arises from the fact that Sebastian doesn't immediately recognize Viola, who is dressed in 'masculine usurped attire'. And anagnorisis is a basic feature of the traditional detective story. It's what Hercule Poirot does every time he gathers the suspects together in a country house drawing-room or on the deck of the Nile steamer and embarks on what is known in American English as the 'big reveal'.

As noted above, catastrophe initially applied to the turn of events that leads to an ending, then to the ending itself and, finally, to an ending which is invariably unhappy. 'Catharsis', meaning purging, was not so much a component of tragic drama but rather the effect it was thought to produce on the audience, a kind of psychological and emotional clearing-out. It has a specialized sense in psychotherapy, to describe the release of buried or repressed emotion connected with a long-ago traumatic event.

JARGON

❧ (1386) ❧

O NCE AGAIN, AS WITH **tragedy** (see previous
entry), we find Geoffrey Chaucer as the first
recorded user of an English word. In his cyni-
cal poem *The Merchant's Tale*, about a marriage between
an aging but wealthy knight called January and a young
woman called May, there's a description of the wedding
night during which the elderly husband, stoked up on the
medieval equivalent of viagra, works away until day begins
to break. Then, says Chaucer's narrator, the Merchant, old
January sits up in bed as frisky as a colt:

> *And ful of jargon as a flekked pye* [magpie].
> *The slakke skyn aboute his nekke shaketh*
> *Whil that he sang, so chaunteth he and craketh* [croaks].

This first use of **jargon** in English doesn't carry its modern meaning. As the comparison with the magpie suggests, it denotes 'chatter', 'the twitter of birds', and derives from similar words in other west European languages, such as the Old French *jargoun*. In later use the word equates to 'meaningless talk' or 'gibberish' before arriving at its current sense in the seventeenth century to describe a vocabulary belonging to a specialist field like economics or computing, a vocabulary full of technical terms which are meaningful to insiders but convey nothing to those on the outside, who are likely to be mystified or irritated or both. **Jargon** serves at least two purposes, one practical, one psychological, within a group: it enables its members to communicate more quickly and effectively when they talk about procedures or tools or concepts; and by excluding outsiders it binds them together as members of that group. But, as the origin of the word demonstrates, it is generally pejorative. **Jargon** is technical talk as overheard by the outsider. The word is also an example, one out of many tens of thousands, of an expression whose meaning and application has modified through the centuries. Chaucer would have understood the modern concept of **jargon**, as an exclusive specialist language, but he wouldn't have understood the word in this sense. Nor do we use or understand the word in his sense of 'bird twitter'. Yet the form of the word has remained unchanged over more than six centuries.

LUKE WARME

❧ (1398) ❧

T
HIS IS AN EARLY SPELLING of **lukewarm** or 'tepid',
one of several versions including *leuk-warme* and
lewk warm before it settled into its modern form
in the seventeenth century. The significant point is that
what is now a single word originally appeared either as a
hyphenated term or, as in the 1398 version above, as two
separate ones. Yet both words mean essentially the same
thing, since the Middle English *leuk/lew* is the equivalent of 'warm', and both 'luke' and 'warm' can be traced
back to Old English in different spellings. There seems to
be no strong linguistic reason for this kind of duplication
or tautology, which also occurs in words like 'courtyard'
('yard-yard'), 'pathway' and 'linchpin' ('axle-pin') or
in phrases such as 'subject matter' or 'ways and means'

or 'null and void'. In some cases the duplication may be explained by the fact that one part of the word or phrase derives from an Old English (i.e. Germanic) source and the other from an Old French (i.e. Romance) source. But this doubling also seems to be a more general feature of English, perhaps because of the richness and depth of its vocabulary. I didn't really need to write 'duplication or tautology' a couple of sentences ago, since both words mean much the same. Yet tautology is the more technical term – and a yet more technical one is 'pleonasm' – and so pins down the sense of the first word more precisely. Tautologies abound in modern English: there's no strict logical need for the second word in 'oak tree', or to say that something is 'bought and paid for', or 'over and done with', or to refer to a PIN number (since the N stands for number) or an ATM machine (because the abbreviation means Automated Teller Machine). Yet we do use these repetitions, either out of habit or for the sake of clarity and rhetorical emphasis. 'Over and done with' conveys a greater finality than either part of the phrase would do in isolation, as does 'bought and paid for'.

MANURE

❧ (1416) ❧

WHAT LINKS DUNG WITH a military exercise? Or, to put it another way, what links **manure** with manoeuvre? The answer is that both words derive ultimately from the same French and Latin sources. **Manure**, first appearing in 1416 in a northern English spelling *manour*, meant to 'till the land', and was a borrowing from French, where depending on its date and regional source the verb appeared in slightly different spellings like *manovrer* or *manouvrer*. This in turn was a borrowing from and combination of a Latin noun and verb, *manus* ('hand') and *operare* ('labour'). Manual labour to work the land was required, in a double sense, in the medieval period as in earlier times. Firstly, there was no equipment or machinery except of the most primitive kind to lighten the load and, secondly, such manual labour was a condition of feudal service. **Manure** as a verb described this kind of work. Not until the early sixteenth century is the word recorded in its modern sense of 'dung', 'fertilizer'. The more elevated term 'manoeuvre' comes directly from French into English around the middle of the eighteenth century, in the two senses in which it is still used: the planned movement of troops, and a skilful, sometimes cunning, action or ploy on the part of an individual or an organization. At the root of both **manure** and manoeuvre is the concept of work done by hand: in one case that work was laborious and would have involved spreading dung on tilled soil; in the other, a later French sense of an adroit manual move, perhaps in a game, seems to have been transferred to the skilful, tactical shifting of troops over the landscape.

CABIN

≈ (1440) ≈

CABIN HAD A LATE medieval meaning of 'grotto' or 'animal den', as well as a room on a ship, before it denoted a temporary shelter or rudimentary house. It came across from French (the medieval and modern French for a wooden hut hasn't changed over the centuries: *cabane*). In a tiny example of the give-and-take between neighbouring languages, when the French required a word for the living quarters on a ship or the cockpit of a plane, they borrowed back the English spelling and added an -e: *cabine*. In doing so, they created two slightly differing words to describe different things where, unusually, English has only one.

William Shakespeare was quite fond of the word **cabin**, generally using it as a noun in the shipboard context. But he followed some earlier writers in using it as a verb as well. When Macbeth learns that the hired murderers he has sent to kill Banquo and his son Fleance have let the boy get away, an escape which may fulfil the witches' predictions that Banquo and not Macbeth will father a line of future kings, he expresses his fear and frustration: 'But now I am cabined, cribbed, confined, bound in/To saucy doubts and fears.' The alliterative, tight-vowelled sounds of cabined, cribbed, confined, all essentially meaning the same thing, echo Macbeth's sense of panicky imprisonment.

The point I want to make here, though, isn't a poetic but a linguistic one. Shakespeare's use of a noun as a verb is an age-old process, one sometimes referred to now as 'verbing', a word which is itself an illustration of the thing it describes. English style and usage guides have long deplored the tendency to transform nouns to verbs, seeing it as an abuse of language. For example, look at Simon Heffer's characteristic injunction in *Simply English: An A–Z of Avoidable Errors* (2014): '*Access* is a noun and not a verb. "Can I access your website?" is a solecism: either say "Can I gain access?" or "Can I see?"' But there is nothing wrong with turning nouns into verbs. The result may not be euphonious, it may even be ugly, but that is a matter of taste not correctness. So, current noun-to-verb examples like 'to action' and 'to impact' and 'to medal' (for 'award medals to') might offend delicate ears; but consider that many other words (like rain and contact and bottle) were nouns long before they turned into verbs, and that those uses now offend no one. What Shakespeare's use of **cabin** as a verb rather than a noun goes to show is that English is a resilient, versatile and elastic language, under the command of its many hundreds of millions of users, whether they happen to be you, me or Shakespeare. What English is not, fortunately, is a servant at the beck and call of those who write guides on how to use it.

MORGAGE

⁓ (c.1450) ⁓

THIS IS ONE OF the early spellings of mortgage, then as now a legal term for the conveyance (i.e. transfer) of land or property to a creditor as security for the fulfillment of some condition, usually the repayment with interest of the loan required to buy the land or property in the first place. **Morg(t)age** comes from French and is a combination of two words, the Latinate *mort* ('dead') and the Old French *gage* ('pledge'). The idea of providing something valuable as a token or pledge that you will do what you promise to do also lies at the heart of 'engage' and 'engagement'. The 'death' bit of mortgage makes the word seem more grim than it really is. The reference is not to the purchaser being in hock until the day he or she dies, but rather to the fact that the agreement itself 'dies' when the mortgagee either pays off the original loan or has the property taken away (foreclosed, repossessed) if the loan cannot be paid off according to whatever conditions were agreed. Despite the ubiquity of the word and the thing itself – how many people can afford to buy a house without taking on a mortgage? (how many young people can afford to buy a house at all now, come to that?) – there are distinct negative overtones to its metaphorical use. Talk of mortgaging one's soul, the future, our children's future, always implies a bad bargain.

ACCELERATION

~ (1490) ~

THIS FAMILIAR WORD DOESN'T appear in quite such a familiar form in 1490 but as *excelleratioune* in an *OED* citation from 'The records of the Parliaments of Scotland', with the sense of 'speeding up'; the context is the more rapid administration of justice. A few years later **acceleration** takes on its modern spelling in English as used south of the border, rather than Scots.*

---

* Scots is not the same as Gaelic, the old language of the Gaels or the Celtic inhabitants of the Highlands and Islands. Scots is rather a descendant of the dialect form of Old English known as Northumbrian, which slowly took on different forms and identities depending on whether the speakers lay north or south of the border. A very substantial part of Scots vocabulary would still baffle English speakers and other words are only half-familiar. The opening line of Robert Burns' famous poem 'To a Mouse' gives examples of both: 'Wee, sleekit, cow'rin, tim'rous beastie'. 'Wee' and 'beastie' are obvious, but 'sleekit' ('sleek', and therefore crafty) is not so well known.

The source for both versions, and for very similar words in other European languages like French, Spanish and Italian is the Latin noun *acceleratio* (in turn from the verb *accelerare*: 'to quicken'). There seems to have been no very precise equivalent for the word – or for the idea of continuously increasing movement in Old English – which explains why it was necessary to borrow from Latin via French to supply the gap. The use of **acceleration** in a scientific sense, for example to describe planetary motion, doesn't occur until the later seventeenth century. The 'accelerator' makes a surprisingly early debut in English in 1611, but it applies not to a mechanism but to a person who hastens matters. The same word described a primitive form of bicycle because it was a machine that would 'accelerate' your normal walking pace, a similar idea to that behind another early term for bicycle, the 'velocipede' ('swift' + 'foot', ultimately from Latin). The automobile application of accelerator is first found in 1900.

FUCK

∼ (EARLY 1500S) ∼

I WAS THERE WHEN THE word, at the time the ultimate four-letter word, was first uttered on British television. Not there literally in the TV studio but sitting at home late in the evening of Saturday 13 November 1965 and watching *BBC-3*, a successor programme to *That Was The Week That Was* (or *TW3*), the programme which launched David Frost and helped to usher in the satire boom of the 1960s. *BBC-3*, so called because there'd been another late-night satire series coming between it and *TW3*, was hosted by Robert Robinson, a cosier and smoother figure than the thrusting youngish Frostie. One of the guests on that notorious 13 November was Kenneth Tynan, best known for his acerbic theatre criticism, and then in the process of becoming Laurence Olivier's right-hand man in the early years of the National Theatre. Later he would make a lot of money out of staging the erotic revue *Oh Calcutta!** though not at the National Theatre. Tynan was plenty of other more elusive things too: a dandy and provocateur, a wit and a *bon vivant*. (His taste for sado-masochism wouldn't really become known until after his premature death in 1980.) He was appearing on *BBC-3* to discuss obscenity, and particularly in relation to a play called *Saved* by Edward Bond, which had been banned from public presentation on the English stage by the Lord Chamberlain. If some of these details make the mid-1960s sound like another era, then that's because in many respects it was another era.

But Ken Tynan was really appearing on *BBC-3* to give vent to a single word. The move was as carefully planned as a military manoeuvre. He wrapped up his monosyllabic four letters so that it sat snugly in the middle of a sentence. He said: 'I doubt if there are any rational people to whom the word "fuck" would be particularly diabolical, revolting or totally forbidden.' Like most television at the time, the show was transmitted live so there was no possibility of editing out or bleeping over his remark. It wasn't taped

---

* *Oh Calcutta!* is a humorously slurred version of a French sex compliment – '*Oh, quel cul tu as!*' ('Wow, what an arse you've got!') – though the person paying the compliment would have to be pretty sure of his (or maybe her) recipient before saying it. *Cul* is a French colloquialism for bottom, rear, backside, and that may be the reason why *cul de sac* to indicate a road without any exit is not used in France itself. Instead, the phrase on signs is *voie sans issue*.

either, which is the reason why that moment has never been seen since. As far as I remember, there was almost no reaction among the discussion panel. Everyone behaved as though the emergence of *those* four letters was the most normal thing in the world. But afterwards, oh that was a different story. The BBC apologized. There were newspaper headlines and angry editorials, all of which could only hint at what Tynan said, and almost a quarter of all MPs signed motions of censure in the House of Commons. Surely, there must have been a few people around in 1965 who could remember the fuss over George Bernard Shaw's deployment of 'bloody' in *Pygmalion* in 1914, a similarly deliberate use of a taboo word to Tynan's fifty years later (see page 180). If so, the mood of national outrage would have seemed very familiar.

At school on the Monday morning after *that* Saturday, the subject reared its head. It was double English. Our teacher was a remarkable man, Frank Miles, FRM. He shared more than his first two initials with the austere, high-minded F. R. Leavis, the doyen, maverick and martyr of the Cambridge English school. Frank Miles was inclined to use words like 'nugatory' and 'velleities'. A reading list from him might contain a Virginia Woolf novel and Joyce's *Ulysses*, in the days when it still had to be produced from under the counter at the public library. Frank and his standards were something to live up to, and the task was undertaken with devotion by those pupils lucky enough to come under his influence. Naturally, Frank did not have a television so could not have seen *BBC-3* – he wouldn't have watched it anyway – but he was an assiduous reader of the papers. 'So what was it that Kenneth Tynan said?' he wanted to know. Eyes were averted, adolescent cheeks took on a pink tinge, no one said a word. So Frank embarked on an anecdote, which for all I know he may have invented. A junior school teacher went round her class, asking for the first thing their daddies said when they got home from work. 'Hello, darling' and 'Have you had a nice day?' and their variants followed until the teacher got to a little girl who claimed that her father's first words on coming through the front door were: 'Fuck off. I'm tired and I need a drink.' Was *that* the word Tynan used? Eyes still turned aside, faces still warm, some of us mumbled yeses or nodded. We talked about it afterwards, Frank's class, still shocked – but also somehow surprised and delighted – that an adult had used the word. The consensus was that we shouldn't mention it to anyone outside the circle, though. Frank might get into trouble. The word was that powerful, that dangerous, even though it had been legal for five years.

The first extensive public outing of **fuck** famously occurred in 1960 when Penguin Books was prosecuted for its publication of D. H. Lawrence's novel *Lady Chatterley's*

Lover. The failure of the prosecution was a watershed. D. H. Lawrence (1885–1930) knew that *Lady Chatterley* was unpublishable in his lifetime because of its sexual explicitness and frequent use of four-letter words. Originally printed privately in Italy in 1928 and sent to subscribers in Britain, the titled lady lived underground for many years until in 1959 the New York Court of Appeals upheld a federal judge's decision that the book had literary merit. This encouraged Penguin to publish the book in the UK, even though they knew they would be prosecuted in a 'test case by arrangement', intended to clarify the obscenity laws.

In case anyone missed it, the book describes a passionate affair between Constance Chatterley, an upper-class woman, and Mellors, a gamekeeper on her husband's estate. Part of the book's shock value lay in this sexual crossing of class boundaries, but the greater part came from Lawrence's description of 'thirteen episodes of sexual intercourse' and the taboo-breaking use of four-letter terms. In the event, the defence's star-studded array of witnesses was hardly required. The prosecution called only one witness: a detective inspector who testified that the book had actually been published. The most famous moment from the case is not an example of Lawrence's four-lettered prose but two sentences from prosecuting counsel Mervyn Griffith-Jones: 'Is it a book that you would wish to have lying around the house? Is it a book you would even wish your wife or servants to read?'

The jury to whom he posed these questions included a furniture-maker, a dock-worker and a teacher. Within a year of its official publication in Britain *Lady Chatterley's Lover* had sold more than two million copies.

Now **fuck** and its offspring like 'fucking' are everywhere. Although bleeped out on television, especially before the 9 p.m. watershed, or asterisked in most newspapers, the tolerance for the word and its place in what one might call public discourse is remarkably high. A few media outlets seem to make a point of using it (step forward the *Guardian*). A telling illustration of changing attitudes to **fuck** and all its derivatives came in 2012 when a row blew up at the gated entrance to Downing Street (see also **Watergate**, page 338). The police guard on duty refused to open the main gate to the then government chief whip Andrew Mitchell so he could take his bicycle through. Instead he was expected to make his exit through the pedestrian gate. Mitchell lost his temper and later conceded that he did say: 'I thought you guys were supposed to fucking help us.' The police log, as reported in several newspapers, had a rather more elaborate tirade, one which Mitchell always denied. His alleged words, according to the *Daily Telegraph*, were: 'Best you learn your f— place...you don't run this f— government... You're f— plebs.' Two years later the affair climaxed in a libel trial, instigated by Andrew Mitchell but also lost by him when the judge declared: 'For the reasons given, I'm satisfied, at least on the balance of probabilities that Mr Mitchell did speak the words attributed to him, or so close to them as to amount to the same, the politically toxic word pleb.'

The significant point from a linguistic perspective, and from a cultural/historical one too, is that thirty or forty years ago Andrew Mitchell would have been lambasted, and perhaps lost his job, for saying 'fucking' to a police-man just the once, let alone repeatedly. Now, by contrast, an apology would have been enough to exonerate him. The word is common, (almost) everybody uses it, there's noth-ing to see here, move along please. In a linguistic twist, it is the word 'pleb' which has become truly offensive, 'polit-ically toxic' in the judge's words, even though until quite recently it would surely have passed unremarked as noth-ing more than a typical upper-crust boorish put-down.

Certainly the British, or the English anyway, have a taste for the word. As noted above, the *Guardian* newspaper is a dedicated employer. As well as intermittent appearances on the mainstream TV channels, it is to be heard regularly on minority ones like BBC4 or Channel 4, whose audiences are assumed to be *blasé* – or small – enough to cope with it. It's standard for an American guest on a Brit chat-show to say something like 'Can I say that?' about various four-letter words and to be assured by the sometimes smug host/inter-viewer that, sure, you can say what you like over here.

The sub-text is: we're not an uptight, prudish bunch like you Yanks. It's perhaps not altogether unjust that one of the slang terms the French have for the English is '*les fuck-offs*.'

There have been some absurd attempts to explain the origins of **fuck**. The silliest explanation of all is that it is some kind of acronym, and suggestions have ranged from Fornication Under Consent of the King (because in ye olde times the king's permission was required for single people to have sex) to File Under Carnal Knowledge (supposedly how Scotland Yard marked rape files).* The likely answer is much more straightforward. It's probably a word inherited from the German, says the *OED*, citing a number of similar-looking terms from early Dutch and various Scandinavian languages with meanings varying from 'have sex with' to 'strike' to 'be tossed by the wind'. John Florio, a contemporary of Shakespeare and an early lexicographer, included it in an Italian–English dictionary, where he gives some English equivalents for the Italian *fottere*, including one used by Chaucer (*swive*), one by Shakespeare (occupy) – and **fuck**.

---

*   A similarly ludicrous etymology hangs around the source of 'shit', the word being attributed to the historical transport by ship of large quantities of manure. If stored low in the ship, it got wet, began to ferment and produce methane gas. Contact with a naked flame destroyed several ships in this manner before anyone worked out what was happening. After that, the bundles of manure were stamped with 'Ship High In Transit', an instruction to stow well above the lower decks so as to protect the cargo from water and the production of methane. Thus, the acronym 'shit'. Which pretty well describes this theory.

An indication of the word's power, whether as slang for sexual activity or as a simple swear-word, is that after Florio's time it pretty well drops out of the record for the next few hundred years. Everybody except the very young or the innocent must have known it, while quite a few people would have been using it in speech, particularly in all-male company, but nobody put it down on paper. Or, if they did, the result was never preserved or published. By the early twentieth century, though, it could be hinted at. In his semi-autobiographical novel *Sons and Lovers* (1913), D.H. Lawrence has this:

> You shouldn't funk [flinch from] your own deeds, man,' remonstrated the friend.
>
> Then Dawes made a remark which caused Paul to throw half a glass of beer in his face.

Most readers would understand that Dawes has said something punning on funk and **fuck** but had Lawrence put this directly in his manuscript, the publisher would have insisted on its removal. When Norman Mailer wrote *The Naked and the Dead* (1948), his classic novel about the war in the Pacific, he euphemized the word by putting 'fug'. A well-known story has the first-time author approached by the actress Tallulah Bankhead: 'Oh, hello, you're Norman Mailer. You're the young man that doesn't know how to spell fuck.'

As a kind of footnote, I'd add that the word or its equivalents don't carry quite such a charge in other European languages. I remember an elderly French woman, a retired teacher, explaining why you shouldn't pour boiling water on the coffee in a cafetière, but rather use the water just before it comes to the boil. (She was right, by the way.) Otherwise, she said, the coffee would be *foutu* – or fucked.

DUNCE

❦ (1531) ❦

HERE IS A WORD that once had positive associations but then turned a historical somersault and took on an opposite meaning. John Duns (*c.*1266–1308), born in Duns (now the county town of Berwickshire) and generally known as Duns Scotus, was a medieval philosopher and theologian. He was sufficiently famous for the refinement and distinction of his thinking to earn the soubriquet of 'Doctor Subtilis'; his work was studied at Oxford and Cambridge, with his disciples being called Scotists. His followers, however intelligent, later came to be regarded by the reformers and humanists of the Renaissance as pedants, hair-splitters and stick-in-the-muds. So in 1531 William Tyndale, the reformer and biblical translator, calls them '*old barkynge curres*' and '*childern of darknesse*', and the term **dunce** (sometimes 'duns') becomes a description of someone who is resistant to new ideas and slow to learn. In 1728 Alexander Pope produced his long satirical poem *The Dunciad*, a jubilant attack on the dullness and stupidity that reigned in London's literary world and across society as a whole.

The dunce's cap, the conical hat sometimes emblazoned with a large capital D, doesn't appear until later, though by 1841, when Charles Dickens published *The Old Curiosity Shop*, it must have been part of the regular equipment of the schoolroom. Little Nell and her grandfather are given hospitality by a poor schoolmaster in whose room among other things: 'on hooks upon the wall in all their terrors, were the cane and ruler; and near them, on a small shelf of its own, the dunce's cap, made of old newspapers and decorated with glaring wafers of the largest size.' The counterpart to the dunce's cap is the 'thinking cap', a phrase that emerged early in the Victorian period. It is almost certainly related to the 'considering cap', an imaginary item of wear first mentioned in 1600 in a book by Robert Armin, who played the clown roles in Shakespeare's acting company.

GOOSEBERRY

∽ (1533) ∼

THOUGH LANGUAGE IS RARELY logical it is, sometimes, quite inexplicable. The Italian for **gooseberry** is *uva spina* ('grape' + 'thorn/prickle'), which makes sense both as an example of word formation and as a description. But the English equivalent doesn't fit into either of these categories; no one can really explain how the word came about or tease out any connection with the goose. Perhaps it's a corruption of an old German term (*krausbeere*) or an early form of the French word *groseille*?* Perhaps it derives from a now-lost English word like 'gorseberry', which would certainly describe

---

* The current French for the fruit is *groseille à maquereau*, because as a sauce it has long been a traditional accompaniment to mackerel.

the fruit more accurately but whose existence can only be hypothecated since there is no record of such a term anywhere? No one knows. Almost as obscure are a couple of gooseberry-related phrases. An old-fashioned reply to a child's question about where it comes from – 'from under the gooseberry bush' – probably hints at a slang sense of 'gooseberry bush' for pubic hair. To 'play gooseberry' is to be a generally unwanted companion/chaperone to a courting couple, to be a 'fifth wheel' in the American expression. But why play the *gooseberry*? It's not the most obvious or the handiest fruit to pick if you're rambling around in pursuit of a young couple. Conceivably, it may be related to another old expression 'to play old gooseberry', meaning to 'cause trouble', 'make a disturbance'. Again, no one knows for certain.

FALL

❧ (1545) ❧

I T WAS AN AUSTRALIAN who coined the expression
'cultural cringe' shortly after the Second World War
to describe the assumption of national writers and
other artists that whatever they produced would necessarily be inferior to anything coming out of the 'mother
country' of Britain, and probably out of other European
nations too. Fortunately, the cringe disappeared in the
next decade or so, as writers and critics like Germaine
Greer, Clive James and Robert Hughes showed just what
Australia could do to, and for, the old country. In the early
days, English speakers in America were also afflicted by
the nervous habit of looking over their shoulders for a nod
of linguistic approval from the very nation against which
they were fighting for independence. But the new country

soon asserted its autonomy and selfhood in several ways, not the least of which was the compiling by Noah Webster of a dictionary published in 1828 and containing distinctively American spellings (center, theater, defense, color, honor). Just how far the US way of speaking and writing the language has come to occupy a predominant position in the world is illustrated by the fact that now, as I type a word such as 'colour' in the British English style, Microsoft Word's spellcheck will query my version with a minatory underlining of red.

It's taken the British a couple of centuries to adjust to this sense that their version of English is overshadowed, even under threat. You'll still hear people deploring the influence of America and Americanisms on British English as if their personal property was at risk, even though the language doesn't 'belong' to them or to anybody else. The situation used to be worse, and not so long ago either. In *Mother Tongue* (1990), Bill Bryson quotes a member of the House of Lords saying in a 1978 debate: 'If there is a more hideous language on the face of the earth than the American form of English, I should like to know what it is.' And the complaints continue, even if not quite so stridently expressed; a letter to *The Times* (4 March 2016) appeared under the heading 'American English' and opened: 'Just because those outside this country choose to attack the English language by inventing such ugly noun-verbs as "weaponising" does not mean that we have to go along with it.' The writer was objecting to the use of the phrase 'deliberately weaponising migration' by a US general on a visit to the UK and claiming that he didn't understand what the speaker meant. Perhaps the expectation is that the American military should start talking British English the moment their feet touch British soil. Or, if they fail to do this, then maybe it's up to newspapers and other media to repair the deficiency by translating their words.

In fact, it's more than likely that the *Times* letter-writer did understand what the general meant or, if he did not, that the context would have made it clear. The real problem is not one of (mis)understanding but rather a kind of aesthetic objection, in this case to the 'ugliness' of 'weaponising', the apparent breaking of some (non-existent) rule that governs the way nouns are turned into verbs, and perhaps a general unease about the supposed American colonization of British English. These are old complaints and anxieties, yet ones that still cause occasional twinges. The truth is that the vigor ('vigour') and sassiness ('self-assurance', 'impudence') of American English have enriched the language on both sides of the Atlantic and around the world, and will continue to do so.

One of the ironies of the fuss about Americanisms is that quite a few of the words objected to as ugly or unnecessary interlopers actually came from Britain in the first place but were forgotten about in the country of origin. Take **fall** in the autumnal sense and deriving from an old Germanic word. It first appears in a seasonal context in 1545 as 'fall of the leaf', in a book on archery dedicated to Henry VIII, and then simply as **fall** in later use. The word migrates with the early settlers, largely replaced by the French-derived 'autumn'. It doesn't leave English shores for good, however, and can be glimpsed in the phrases 'spring and fall' and 'the fall of the year'. Other examples of words which have been transported and sometimes returned include: 'diaper', the US version of nappy but used for a small towel or cloth from the early seventeenth century in England, and 'faucet', standard American for a tap, but with a similar English meaning well before Columbus discovered the New World. 'Guess' and 'trash' are two more examples of supposed Americanisms. *Gesse* appears in Chaucer's *The Canterbury Tales*, dating from the mid-fourteenth century and with much the same sense as the modern US English of 'suppose' or 'imagine' – of the Knight's Squire, Chaucer says '*Of twenty yeer of age he was, I gesse.*' 'Trash' takes on the sense of 'refuse' or 'something unwanted' in 1555. Fifty or so years later in the tragedy of *Othello* Iago says: 'Who steals my purse steals trash; 'tis something, nothing.' The first recorded US usage of 'trash' meaning 'rubbish to be put out' comes 400 years after that. Now it's crept – or snuck – back into British English. Some American pronunciations are also relics of older, discarded British English styles of speech. The characteristic US sounding of *erb* for 'herb' echoes the Middle English word form, *erbe*; similarly, the American pronunciation of 'not' is closer to the Middle English *nat*.

The trickle of American terms into British English will continue, newer terms joining long-established expressions that have more or less replaced the 'native' ones, such as apartment (instead of 'flat') or elevator ('lift'). Sometimes it's a question of whole phrases. Younger British English speakers especially are more likely to employ expressions like 'left field', to describe any source from which unexpected things might emerge, or to refer to 'a whole new ballpark' where older speakers might say something like 'a different kettle of fish'. Also from baseball come 'stepping up to the plate' (entering the batter's area and so a metaphor for 'taking control', 'rising to a challenge') and 'ballpark figure' for an approximate number. A range of other terms are far from established and occupy a position somewhere in the Atlantic, perhaps closer to US shores than British ones; among these one might include the US navy 'scuttlebutt' ('gossip, rumour'), 'bloviate' ('speak pompously'), and 'boilerplate' meaning formulaic, and usually applied to clichéd prose or a standard form of document such as a contract. If ever these terms do become fixed in British English, there will probably be the odd rumble of protest. But even for those so inclined, there is nothing they can really do about such imports. The notion of 'fighting back' against so-called ugly or unwelcome linguistic arrivals is not only a waste of time but betrays a basic ignorance about how language operates. The worldwide community of English is the ultimate free-trade area. There are no sniffer dogs, no border checks, no quotas, no tariffs, no protectionist policies, nothing at all which will be effective in keeping out the intruders. This is good news.

BONA FIDE

OST WORDS THAT ARE imported into English from other languages – i.e. the words that make up the vast majority of our own language – undergo a process of alteration and assimilation that changes them, not perhaps out of all recognition, but into a form markedly different from their source. But some words and phrases survive the import business intact. They are still wrapped in their original packaging, so to speak, just as when they first arrived. French and Latin provide the bulk of such expressions. A Latin example appears in the very first sentence of this paragraph: i.e. (*id est*: 'that is (to say)'). And, of course, an example is frequently signalled in writing with the Latin abbreviation e.g. (*exempli gratia*: 'for the sake of an example'). A feature of these expressions is that they *never* appear in full.

Latin also gives us **bona fide**, literally 'in/with good faith' and first cited in this sense in an Act of Parliament in Henry VIII's time. Now the phrase tends to be used adjectivally to mean 'genuine', 'authentic' ('Are food bloggers always bona fide?'). There's also a noun form, **bona fides**, meaning 'good faith' in a legal context – as opposed to with fraudulent intentions – and which more generally conveys the idea of things being above board ('They showed identity cards to prove their bona fides.'). Let's stick with the word for a moment since *bonus*, the Latin for 'good' and the source for bonus in a financial sense, gives us a couple more expressions. *Cui bono (est)?* means 'For whose good is it?' or 'Who stands to profit?', and is sometimes used to point the finger of blame. If a crime has been committed for some gain or advantage and the perpetrator's identity is in doubt, a detective with a bit of Latin and no regard for his street cred might ask '*Cui bono?*' Such a phrase, though, is much more likely to emerge from a lawyer's lips in court. And lawyers, especially in the US, are very familiar with the expression *pro bono publico* or 'for the public good' since pro bono work is a legal task undertaken without pay, as in 'Mrs Blair has strongly rejected the position of Mrs Clooney, who is working pro bono on Mr Nasheed's case' (*Daily Telegraph*).

Because the legal system of ancient Rome had a shaping effect on the legal systems of many Western countries, it's not surprising that there is an age-old nexus ('link', in Latin) between the law and Latin. The link survives in quite a few terms in modern English. In addition to *cui bono?* and *pro bono*, we find familiar expressions like *habeas corpus* and *affidavit* as well as the specialist terms *ad litem* or *amicus curiae*, applying to people with some supervisory responsibility in law. *Alias* and *alibi* are both borrowings from Latin, as is the simple *v.* or *vs.* standing for *versus* and separating the opposed parties in court cases.

ALCHOCOL

❧ (1543) ❧

THIS FAMILIAR-LOOKING WORD IS indeed 'alcohol', as it appears in its first citation in English ('The barbarous* auctours [authors] use alchohol') in a book about surgery translated from Latin. The word does not have the meaning that attaches to it today. Alcohol's debut in English is a chemical one, denoting a powder obtained by grinding, and deriving from the Arabic *al + kuhl*, literally 'the' + 'powder' (as in *kohl*, traditionally used in the East to darken the eyes). The word could also apply to a liquid produced by distillation as well as

---

* The 'barbarous' authors referred to are Moorish or Arabic. In this context 'barbarous' (see Barbarian, page 104) is a relatively neutral term, conveying not much more than 'foreign'.

a powder, the common elements being ideas of concentration and refinement. Then the word begins to get closer to its modern sense in the seventeenth-century phrase 'alcohol of wine', even if a slightly technical air still clings to it. But not until the beginning of the nineteenth century does 'alcohol' come to stand by itself as a shorthand term to represent any one of a large number of intoxicating liquids. Now alcohol and its many dependent offshoots, whether in the form of abbreviations (AA/Alcoholics Anonymous) or slang (alky) or commercial (alcopop) or formal usage ('alcohol awareness'), have all established themselves in modern English. A tenuous link between the old chemical/medicinal sense of alcohol and the current one is provided not only by the supposed steadying, fortifying or health-giving effects of some drinks (brandy, stout, red wine) but by the word 'tincture'.

The prefix *al-* ('the') can be an indicator of words derived historically from Arabic, often via Spanish, because of the North African Moorish occupation of the country in the early Middle Ages. Other examples include: alcove, algebra, alchemy, alembic, alkali, *alcatras* ('pelican') – the source of the name of the island and one-time prison in San Francisco Bay – and probably the related albatross. Spanish place-names such as Alicante, Algeciras and Alhambra show the same identifying feature. The *al-* definite article, no longer a prefix, is also detectable in 'arsenal', from Arabic for 'workshop', itself made up of three words meaning literally 'place of art/industry' (*dar al-cina'a*), and originally applying to a dockyard and then an armoury.

BUM

⁓ (1547) ⁓

AFTER SAMUEL JOHNSON PUBLISHED his *Dictionary of the English Language* (see **Lexicographer**, page 170), a lady approached him with congratulations not on the words that he had included in the dictionary but on the ones which he had left out:

> A literary lady expressing to Dr. J. her approbation of his Dictionary and, in particular, her satisfaction at his not having admitted into it any improper words; 'No, Madam,' replied he, 'I hope I have not daubed my fingers. I find, however that you have been looking for them.'

Or so the story goes. There are several differing versions, a couple of which have the lady not complimenting

Johnson for his discretion but complaining because he *had* included improper words. His reply, though the wording varies slightly, is always to the effect that she could only know this if she had been searching for them. In fact, in his *Dictionary* published in 1755, Samuel Johnson did cover a handful of terms generally described as 'not in polite use', to use the expression sometimes employed by the contemporary *Oxford English Dictionary*. Among Johnson's inclusions in this category are: *piss* ('Urine; animal water'/'To make water'), *fart** ('Wind from behind'), *turd* ('Excrement'), *arse* ('The buttocks') and *bum* ('The buttocks; the part on which we sit').

Bum has quite an old pedigree, even if it's not as antique as 'arse', which – in a different spelling – goes back over a thousand years. No one is sure of its origin though linguistic speculation makes a connection with 'bump', in the sense of a protuberance. ('Bump', signifying a blow, is onomatopoeic; then the word seems to get transferred to the 'swelling' which is the result of such a blow.) From its earliest days, the buttock word was used as an insult, as in the expressive Scottish 'blaitie bum'. The sense of 'tramp', which originated in the US in the middle of the nineteenth century, does not come from the posterior **bum** but more

---

*   *Fart* is illustrated in the *Dictionary* with this ditty by the Restoration poet John Suckling, as chosen by Johnson: 'Love is the fart / Of every heart; / It pains a man when 'tis kept close; / And others doth offend, when 'tis let loose.'

probably from a *bummer* or idler (German *Bummler*: 'stroller, dawdler'). The American equivalent for the body-part **bum**, a term which is for colloquial rather than formal use, is 'butt', a return to the source word for 'buttock' (i.e. an offshoot of butt, as in the thicker end of an implement or a weapon). In addition, 'ass' is the general US usage for 'arse' in British English.

Unsurprisingly, considering its multiple angles, whether considered functionally, aesthetically, erotically or shamefully, there is a plethora of terms to describe the human bottom. There are what one might call positional descriptions such as 'backside', 'behind', 'rear (end)', 'seat', 'posterior', 'bottom', 'fundament'; there are ones with faintly animal overtones such as 'hindquarters', 'rump', 'haunches'; and then the half-humorous 'cheeks', 'buns' and *derrière*. American English abounds in slang terms, including 'booty' (probably from 'botty'), 'keister'(?), 'tail', 'can' (also slang for lavatory), 'duff' ('dough?'), 'heinie' (diminutive of 'behind'), 'tush/tushy' (from Yiddish *tochus*: 'buttocks').

All of this makes British English, with its simple **bum** and arse, as well as its occasional duff and its imported booty, look somewhat undernourished. And that's before we even arrive at 'fanny', which deserves a paragraph to itself. George Bernard Shaw supposedly described England and America as two countries divided by a common language, even if the statement is nowhere to be found in his prolific writings. But if he *had* said it, then it would never be more true than of fanny. In the US it has been a slang term for the buttocks since at least the early twentieth century, but in Britain the word has been slang for the vagina from the mid-Victorian period. The travel item known as the 'bumbag' in the UK is referred to as a 'fanny pack' in the US, a possible source of confusion.* The source of the term, whether applied to the back or front, is unknown. It's been suggested that the British version derives from John Cleland's erotic eighteenth-century work *Fanny Hill: Memoirs of a Woman of Pleasure*, although this seems unlikely as the novel was prosecuted and suppressed for most of its existence and never achieved the notoriety of, say, *Lady Chatterley's Lover*. What is possible is that Cleland was making a punning genital reference in the full name of his heroine, Fanny Hill. If this is the case, then the pre-existing slang British 'fanny' is considerably more ancient than the American one.

---

* The possibilities for linguistic misunderstandings between British and US speakers are generally overstated but they do exist. When Louise Rennison, author of *Angus, Thongs and Full-Frontal Snogging*, was doing a promotional tour in America she mentioned 'lighting a fag'. The journalist interviewing her was shocked: 'Don't you think that's kind of cruel?'

BARBARIAN

≈ (c.1550) ≈

A N EARLY USE OF **barbarian** in the King James translation of the Bible (1611) gives an idea of the original significance of the word. In the First Letter to the Corinthians, Paul writes: 'Therefore if I know not the meaning of the voice, I shall be unto him that speaketh, a Barbarian, and he that speaketh shall be a Barbarian unto me.' Here **barbarian** signifies no more than someone who doesn't understand your language, just as you don't understand his. For the ancient Greeks the term βάρβαρος ('barbarous') was applied to non-Greek speakers, possibly growing out of an onomatopoeic attempt to imitate the babbling sound of such a speaker. The word might also derive from an old Arabic verb meaning to 'speak noisily and confusedly'. For the Greeks and Romans, the **barbarian** was, by the very fact of not understanding them, someone who lived untouched by the blessings of their civilizations, and therefore someone uncultured, primitive.

While **barbarian** might have once been a neutral description of someone you didn't understand, it soon took on negative overtones. But then any piece of 'foreign' terminology in English, whether applicable to a race or tribe or sometimes an individual, is likely to move rapidly from the purely descriptive to the pejorative. This is especially the case when it comes to words denoting ethnicity. During the Elizabethan age and long afterwards, the ethnic sense of Turk ran in tandem with other more negative ones, suggestive of savagery. Turkey, or rather the Ottoman empire, lay at the edge of Christian Europe and threatened it too. 'To turn Turk' was to become a renegade, i.e. to defect from Christianity. At different periods of history, 'Arab' has been a disparaging term, while in Victorian London homeless children were called street arabs. To venture into the fraught history of the word 'Jew' is to find oneself in a linguistic minefield, but it is fair to say that, throughout history, Jew has been used much more often in a pejorative sense than it has in a purely descriptive one. At a lesser level, and from a different continent, the American Indian Mohawks had their name appropriated in the eighteenth century by an aristocratic 'race of rakes', referred to as Mohocks, and sounding like a violent proto-Bullingdon Club. A century later the term 'apache', initially appearing in French, meant a street thug.

None of the Germanic tribes whose incursions into the Roman empire contributed to its eventual downfall has enjoyed a good press. The Vandals, who took and sacked Rome in AD 455, are synonymous with wilful destruction, even if the word as it is currently used in English (e.g., 'a vandal-proof bus-shelter') does not quite suggest the destruction of the Eternal City. The Goths were similarly equated with barbarism, though the word developed much more elaborate, interesting and ambivalent off-shoots. The Gothic style of architecture was apparently so named to distinguish it from the classical Greek and Roman styles, and from the seventeenth century the word appears in different spellings such as *Gothique, Gotique* (as in French) and *Gothick*, and begins to be applied to poetry and prose as well. As such, it turns into a term that is both threatening and alluring. Ken Russell's 1986 film farrago about the tangled lives of Shelley, Mary Shelley and Lord Byron at the Villa Diodati on the shores of Lake Geneva in the summer of 1816 (see **Frankenstein**, page 240) was titled *Gothic*.

And then there are the Huns. When the German Kaiser, Wilhelm II, addressed his troops in 1900 before they embarked for China to join the other Great Powers in suppressing the Boxer rebellion, he commanded them to imitate the behaviour of the Huns 'a thousand years ago, under the leadership of Etzel [German for Attila]'. Already a term of abuse among English speakers, Hun was soon to be added to Bosch and Kraut as derogatory slang for the German enemy, particularly during the First World War. Attila, name-checked by the Kaiser, regularly joins Genghis Khan, and occasionally Ivan the Terrible, as an epitome of brutal, despotic authority, even if there's sometimes humour in the reference – 'He's somewhere to the right of Genghis Khan,' is far from being an insult in some circles.

Non-ethnic nouns and adjectives indicative of 'otherness', even if they started life in a fairly neutral state, quickly tended to slip until they became synonymous with something undesirable and even frightening. 'Outlandish', now carrying the sense of 'odd' or 'outrageous', comes all the way from Old English, and the make-up of the word indicates its primary meaning of 'not from this land', 'not indigenous'. 'Foreign' originally denoted merely what was 'outside', then 'distant', then 'deriving from another country', then 'unfamiliar' and so 'strange'. It's often associated with food. British insularity used to be encapsulated in the outraged cry, 'I'm not eating any of that foreign muck!' Within less than a century 'strange' itself made the same journey from 'of another country' (used in this sense in 1297) to 'unfamiliar' to 'odd'. 'Alien' was once a verb, from Norman French, with the sense of 'make hostile' or 'put at a remove' (now in English 'alienate').* The same word, whether as noun and adjective, was employed from the fourteenth century to signify something or somebody foreign, different and almost certainly unwelcome. This is the most hostile term of them all: enemy aliens are the first people to be rounded up when hostilities break out, because they are nationals of the country with which their host nation is at war. First appearing in the extraterrestrial sense in 1929 as part of the title of a science-fiction story, 'alien' is the colder, more threatening version of ET. That title was just right for Spielberg's 'phone-home' tear-jerker, but Ridley Scott's cold space masterpiece, *Alien* (1979), would hardly have carried the same charge if it had been called 'Stranger' or 'Foreigner'.

On the spectrum of outsiderness, the most extreme terms are now almost obsolete. 'Pagan' springs from Latin *paganus* ('rustic') and probably acquired its sense of 'non-Christian' or 'heathen' from the fact that worship of the old gods persisted in rural areas long after Christianity was generally accepted in the major population centres of the Roman empire. The word first appeared in plural

---

* The *alienist* was the nineteenth-century precursor of the psychiatrist, the term used to describe someone who treated those suffering from mental disorders. It comes from the French (*aliéné*: insane).

form (*payganys*) in *Le Morte Arthure*, an anonymous late fourteenth-century poem about King Arthur, and the first of several works about a figure who had a magical appeal for the knightly and educated classes of the Middle Ages. Similarly to pagan, 'heathen' – from an Old English word – probably denoted an outsider, a 'dweller on a heath', and so an individual more likely to cling to old practices and beliefs. 'Infidel' (or 'unbeliever') could be used either way round, from a Christian point of view applying to Muslims, etc. and from a Muslim point of view applying to Christians, etc. With neat symmetry the first citation in the plural for this word (*infydeles*) occurs in *Le Morte d'Arthur* by Sir Thomas Malory, written half a century or more after the first *Le Morte Arthure*.

There are only a couple of foreign-related words that convey, if not outright approval, then a degree of curiosity about the outside world. One is 'exotic'. Like most other terms here, it originally pointed to what was outside or beyond, from the Greek and Latin roots exo-/ex-, but exotic now hints at something that is glamorous and appealing not despite but *because* of its foreignness. Exotic destinations promise new excitements, while exotic fruits provide a different taste from the familiar apples and pears. And with its one-letter difference from 'erotic' the word is handy in the euphemism 'exotic dancer' for stripper. The other non-pejorative term is 'abroad', in medieval times having the sense of 'over a wide area' or 'publicly' (just about surviving in expressions like 'spread the word abroad'), and by the nineteenth century used only to apply to the world outside one's own country.

UTOPIAN

~ (1551) ~

U TOPIAN IS BORROWED FROM the title of a book
by Sir Thomas More (1475–1535), who was Lord
Chancellor under Henry VIII until his imprisonment, conviction for treason and execution. In *Utopia*,
published in 1516 and formed out of two Greek words
meaning 'not' and 'place', or 'nowhere', More imagined an
island country where a kind of proto-communism pre-
vailed and where there was complete freedom of religion.
Whether he was presenting a picture of an ideal society
or being satirical is still debated, and the current use of
utopian reflects a word that is capable of sitting on both
sides of the fence. It can be used to welcome something
('London 2012 Olympics: a beautiful, utopian, collective
dream', *Guardian* headline) as well as to dismiss something

('Paradoxically, Conservatism is often politics for people who don't like politics – or, at least, who eschew utopian ideology.' *Daily Telegraph*).

It was inevitable that the concept of a utopia, a place where everything is perfect, should spawn its opposite. The only question was what the word would be. 'Dystopia' emerged – rather late in the day one might think, since it was first cited in 1952 – to describe a place where everything, especially the government, is as bad as it might be. Another term exists, 'cacotopia' ('bad place' in Greek), but it is rarely found though *A Clockwork Orange* author Anthony Burgess did his best to popularize it, claiming it was a compound of 'cacophony' and 'utopia'. The prime example of a dys- or cacotopia is George Orwell's *Nineteen Eighty-Four*.* Burgess produced his own version of

---

* Orwell's famous dystopia introduced Big Brother and Room 101 to the world. It's an odd fact that this bleak novel should have produced titles for two of the most popular shows on British television. The looming, sinisterly avuncular figure of Big Brother owed something to Stalin, while 101 was the number of a room in the BBC where Orwell worked in the Second World War. Curiously, it also featured in the real life of the Cambridge spy Guy Burgess. In 1956, some years after Burgess's defection to Moscow, the journalist Richard Hughes was staying at the National Hotel in the city to interview the Soviet foreign minister. He was also seeking information on the fate of Burgess and Donald Maclean. Getting nowhere, he was packing to leave when he received a phone call asking him to come to Room 101. There, Hughes found five men, two of whom introduced themselves as the missing British defectors. Burgess was wearing his Old Etonian tie. In his biography of Burgess, *Stalin's Englishman* (2015), Andrew Lownie speculates that putting the pair in Room 101 of the National Hotel may have been a private joke on the part of the KGB.

the satire by tweaking Orwell's year in one of his lesser novels, *1985*.

Utopian is one of a clutch of words describing imaginary states, regions or landscapes, which have escaped from their fictional borders and been given a wider application in the English language. Jonathan Swift's surreal and satirical novel *Gulliver's Travels* (1726) introduced the land of Lilliput and its six-inch-tall inhabitants. 'Lilliputian' not only connotes extreme smallness but has overtones of pettiness too. The next place Gulliver went to was the land of Brobdingnag, where the people were giants but morally superior to ordinary-sized humans; 'Brobdingnagian' means 'on a great scale' even if the word is rarely found. Other creations from *Gulliver's Travels* have made it into the dictionaries, including 'Struldbrug', an invented name for members of a race who were given immortality but suffered increasing decrepitude as they lived on and miserably on. The final land explored by Lemuel Gulliver is ruled by the 'houyhnhnms', pronounced something like 'hooey-nims' and intended to represent the neighing of a horse, since that is exactly what they are. These intelligent, noble and speaking horses rule over a degraded ape-like race which, being violent, dirty and selfish, naturally represents humanity. It's here that Swift's deftness with names has had an enduring after-life, for the degraded ape-like beings are the 'Yahoos'. For most of its life 'yahoo' was synonymous with words like lout, hooligan and ignoramus. Then in 1994 it was adopted by the creators of the search engine who added an exclamation mark – Yahoo! – and turned an insult into a whoop of triumph. It's been claimed that the word stands for 'Yet Another Hierarchically Organized Oracle' but this is a piece of retrospective fiddling, or a 'backronym' as it's been christened (i.e. an acronym made up *following* the appearance of a word, and so not a true acronym at all). The company name derives ultimately from Jonathan Swift, since yahoo is a dismissive US term like hick or rube for an uncouth countryman, and was apparently applied to one of Yahoo!'s founders by his girlfriend.

Jonathan Swift left a rich linguistic legacy but other writers have done their bit when it comes to imaginary realms. They include 'Wonderland', not coined by *Alice's Adventures in Wonderland* author Lewis Carroll but popularized by him, and an eastern equivalent in 'Shangri-La'. This evocative if faintly naff name, created by James Hilton for his novel *Lost Horizon* (1933) and deriving partly from a Tibetan word for a mountain pass, describes a remote, serene place. (In 1942 President Roosevelt called his wooded retreat in Maryland Shangri-La; it was later renamed Camp David by President Eisenhower, after his grandson.) Now it is the brand name of a luxury hotel chain. Another alluring and fictitious place was 'El Dorado', in Spanish literally 'the gilded', a city on the Amazon packed and paved with gold according to Spanish legend, and in quest of which Walter Raleigh mounted two expeditions.

Even more inaccessible than an Amazonian treasure-city is 'cloud cuckoo land', deriving from Aristophanes's comic play *The Birds* where it features as a realm built by birds to separate the gods from mankind. Now the phrase is used to denote beliefs and ideas that are impractical or delusive. A usage first recorded in 1979, the US 'la-la land' denotes a deluded place, one utterly without self-awareness, bringing together the fantasy film world of Los Angeles or LA and the trilling, inconsequential sound of someone singing 'la la'. Much older and more curious is the land of 'Cockaine', a fabled place of ultimate gluttony and laziness. The word and the notion have been around since the Middle Ages: Pieter Bruegel painted a picture in which roast fowl lay themselves out on platters ready to be eaten and a roof is covered in pies and pastries. The origin of the word is uncertain; a connection with German *kuchen* ('cake') has been suggested. In the nineteenth century, Cockaine was applied humorously to London, as the home of the Cockney. At the turn of the twentieth century and the height of the British Empire, Edward Elgar wrote a piece titled *Cockaigne (In London Town)*, usually referred to as the *Cockaigne Overture*, while in 1928 the US folk singer Harry McClintock recorded 'Big Rock Candy

Mountain', a modernized version of the Land of Cockaine. It's a paradise for bums, hobos and drifters as suggested by lines like 'In the Big Rock Candy Mountain / The cops have wooden legs / The bulldogs all have rubber teeth / And the hens lay soft-boiled eggs.'

Imagined places that have at least a tenuous connection with actual ones include: *Erewhon* (1872), the title of a very readable satire by Samuel Butler and the name of his fictitious country. Erewhon is related to Thomas More's Utopia since the place is, more or less, Nowhere spelled backwards. Butler based the topography of Erewhon in part on New Zealand where he'd spent some years as a sheep farmer. Another antipodean reference is 'never-never land', the perfect country in J. M. Barrie's *Peter Pan*, but applied in Australia in the nineteenth century to the outback. Various novelists have taken real landscapes and made them into fictional territories that have enjoyed a linguistic life outside the page. Anthony Trollope's Barsetshire novels give a picture of a 'pleasant, green, tree-becrowded county', in Trollope's own words; a kind of Victorian counterpart to the county of Borsetshire in Radio 4's long-running *The Archers*. There was a scholarly as well as a fashionable interest in the Anglo-Saxon era during the Victorian period, and both people and town-streets were given Old English names (Hereward, Athelstan, Alfred). But Thomas Hardy went much further and created an entire world in

Wessex – from Old English *West Seaxe* or West Saxons –
in novels like *Far From the Madding Crowd* and *Jude the
Obscure*. It was a world that Hardy described as 'partly real,
partly dream'.

TURKEY

≈ (1555) ≈

THERE IS A CERTAIN irony in the fact that the title of the bird that is a central part of America's Thanksgiving celebrations is essentially a misnomer. Had those early Massachusetts settlers who chased down the wild **turkey** been aware of where it really came from they might have come up with a more appropriate name. The **turkey** is an instance of how, when something has once been named, it is difficult to alter that name even when the facts that led to it being so called have changed. The bird was first domesticated in Mexico, where it was called *huexolotl* from its gobbling noise, but it ran wild in the eastern forests of what became the USA. The first settlers mistakenly identified the **turkey** as being from the same species as an African bird imported into Europe via

118

the Turkish or Ottoman empire. This African-based variety was also known as guineafowl after the Portuguese brought it direct from Guinea in West Africa. The flesh of the American 'turkies' was said to be similar to the birds out of 'New Guiny', which were spotted 'black and white like a Barbers apron'. When the turkeys were eventually sorted out from the guineas, the 'wrong' source-name stuck with the American one.

The bird appears in several metaphorical guises, mostly tending towards the negative, as in 'talking turkey' (to talk business) or going 'cold turkey' (enduring abrupt withdrawal from a drug addiction). The application of 'turkey' to a disastrous film or play may originate in a derisive description of the rustics composing the audience of travelling shows presented by third-rate players who might also be termed 'turkeys'. And it has also been suggested that there's a note of contempt for a bird, once running wild in the untouched forests of the New World, which 'allowed' itself to be tamed, fattened and eaten in celebration of a day marking the beginnings of modern America. Such contempt would entail a degree of self-contempt too. It's no coincidence that one of the most popular brands of bourbon in the US is called Wild Turkey.

SYCOPHANT

≈ (1575) ≈

T HERE ARE QUITE A few abusive synonyms for the flatterer, among them toady, crawler, parasite, lickspittle, bootlicker, time-server and yes-man. The bluntest of them are brown-noser and arse-licker, while the oddest is **sycophant**. Originally having the sense of tale-teller or malicious informer, the **sycophant** swiftly added flattery to his armoury, presumably because such people will readily tell tales in order to ingratiate themselves with authority. Eventually 'flatterer' became the principal definition. The word originates in two Greek terms meaning 'fig' and 'to show' so that a **sycophant** is, etymologically speaking, a 'fig-shower'. Why?

There is a clue in a sixteenth-century translation into English of Plutarch's *Parallel Lives*, a series of biographical sketches of famous Greeks and Romans written in the first century AD, and a source extensively used by Shakespeare for plays such as *Antony and Cleopatra*. Plutarch's fig bit reads (in modernized spelling):

> We may not altogether discredit those which say, they did forbid in the old time that men should carry figs out of the country of Attica [Greece], and that from thence it came that these pick-thanks [flatterers], which betray & accuse them that transported figs, were called Sycophants.

An eighteenth-century commentary fleshed out the picture by claiming that, during a time of food shortage, it became a capital offence to break into someone's garden and steal their figs. But because the punishment was so disproportionate to the crime the informers, the 'fig-showers', were regarded with contempt.

Sadly, such colourful stories seem unlikely to be the right explanation for the **sycophant**. More plausible is that the original Greek word draws on the ages-old symbolism of the fig. Shakespeare has a loud-mouthed character in *Henry V* dismiss another with the words 'Die and be damn'd! and figo for thy friendship!' before invoking the 'fig of Spain'. This gesture involves closing the fingers and sticking the thumb up between two of them. In this non-English equivalent of giving the (middle) finger, the fig/thumb shape conveys a supposed phallic message, and an insulting one at that. But the fig is nothing if not versatile; in Italian, while the noun for the fruit is masculine (*fico*), the feminine form of *fica* is a slang term for the vagina. So it is possible that the **sycophant** or fig-shower or informant is uncovering what he or she shouldn't, exposing others' privacy, or alternatively that the term is an expression of contempt thrown back at those who do so. But these are only two possible explanations, and the word **sycophant** is likely to remain mysterious as to its original meaning.

TULIP

≈ (1578) ≈

T HE WORD FOR THE flower, which was introduced from Turkey in the sixteenth century, is similar across western European languages (Italian: *tulipano*; French: *tulipe*; German: *Tulpe*; Dutch: *tulp*). First appearing in English in such varying forms as *tulpia*, *tulipa* and *tulipant*, it had by the middle of the seventeenth century settled into its modern, recognizable **tulip** shape. An account of the flower in an Elizabethan Herbal (a book detailing the properties of plants) tells of how 'after [it] hath beene some fewe daies flowred, the points and brims of the flower turne backward'. The **tulip**'s bulbous appearance and its Turkish origin explain the name, for the Turks had taken and adapted the Persian term *dulband* ('turban'), applying it to both the headdress and the flower.

The turban itself also went through a variety of spellings, at least one of which (*tulipant*) was the same as the flower, before its form was regularized in English. The 'tulipomania', which swept the Netherlands in the 1630s and which, at its peak, meant that a single bulb might be sold for many times the yearly wages of a skilled craftsman, is generally regarded as the first financial bubble, when the price of an asset rises to a value far beyond its intrinsic worth before a catastrophic plunge. The term 'Tulipomania' appears in English in 1710. The hordes of investors and speculators who went in search of quick profit probably would not have been much concerned that the word 'horde' also derives from Turkish. It was first noted in English in the same period as **tulip**, and originally used to describe the marauding nomadic tribes from the East such as the Tartars but soon took on the more general sense of a 'large gathering', 'pack'.

PROMETHEAN

≈ (1594) ≈

T HE RENAISSANCE PERIOD SAW a new appreciation
of the classical world, its literature and learning,
and its myths. This is reflected in the emergence in
English between the mid-sixteenth and mid-seventeenth
centuries of various eponymous terms relating to the classical gods and legendary heroes. The demi-god Prometheus
(from a Greek word meaning literally 'he who thinks in
advance') stole fire from the gods and taught mankind
how to use it, and also bequeathed to the language the
word **Promethean**, first used in 1594 by George Chapman
in his poem 'The Shadow of Night'; it suggests daring as
well as invention. Another demi-god was Hercules, sired
by Zeus out of a mortal woman Alcmene, to the displeasure of Zeus's wife Hera who vengefully sent Hercules into

a fit of madness during which he killed *his* wife. In atonement Hercules had to perform twelve labours that tested his great or 'Herculean' strength, an adjective first cited in 1610. One of these labours involved cleaning out the dung-filled stables of the king of Augeas, which Hercules achieved by diverting a couple of rivers, in the process giving to English a frequently used phrase ('...old Michel may not be the best bet to clean out the Augean stables of football's governing body,' *Spectator*) with the epithet 'Augean' making its debut in 1599.

Proteus was a sea- and river-god endowed with the gift of prophecy but, to escape being questioned, he kept changing shape. The related adjective 'protean' suggests somebody who is 'changeable', 'multi-faceted', and, as with **Promethean**, George Chapman is again recorded as the first user in 'The Shadow of Night' (1594). Apollo, both a Greek and Roman god, was a multi-tasking figure, with responsibilities ranging from the sun to poetry to medicine. As well as being an exemplar of male beauty, Apollo stands for harmony and control, so that the epithet 'Apollonian' (first cited in 1664) is sometimes contrasted with 'Dionysian' ('drunken', 'orgiastic', from Dionysus, the ancient Greek god of wine, and appearing in English from the early seventeenth century).

'Erotic', a usefully capacious word initially noted in 1668 and covering anything from the mildly sexy to the near-pornographic, takes its cue from the Greek god of love, Eros. The Roman equivalent was Cupid, sometimes depicted in myth as the love child of Venus and Mars (or Aphrodite and Ares in Greece), but under the name of Cupid a rather more cute and cuddly figure than Eros. Venus was goddess of sex, desire, procreation and fertility. She is the source of the now obsolete word *venery*, meaning the pursuit of sexual pleasure, but whose final 1851 citation in the *OED* comes from a dissertation on diseases of the bladder. The adjective 'venereal' is now used only in the context of disease or infection. 'Priapic', meaning 'lustful', 'sex-obsessed', coming from Priapus, a deity originating in Asia Minor and usually sculpted as a dwarfish figure with a vast phallus, standing either aloft or at half-mast, was a quasi-academic term used by the Victorians.

HUM

≈ (1598) ≈

I N *HENRY IV, PART I*, Shakespeare has the hot-blooded Hotspur complaining about his talkative father-in-law: 'I cried hum, and well, go to. But markt him not a word.' Of course, this can't be the first time that **hum** was uttered aloud to signify doubt or hesitation, but rather the first time the *written* use of the word was recorded. It's an example of a particular kind of interjection – others include er, um, hum, hem, h'm – indicating hesitation or scepticism in speech. These interjections (see under **Lackadaisical** for more examples, page 215) are among the oldest sounds of all but they are rarely committed to paper. Why should they be? After all, they are intimately linked to speech, more akin to primitive sounds than articulated words. So it's hardly surprising that the first citation for 'er' in the *OED* is 1862 and although 'um' is significantly earlier (1672) it occurs as part of a line of dialogue in a play.

But like all really useful little words, these simple interjections are capable of development and variation. Adding a 'ho' to the **hum** produces an adjective denoting something average or disappointing ('the ho-hum economy', 'ho-hum titles'), or a more nuanced interjection denoting uncertainty or resignation ('I see the weather forecast is terrible again. Ho-hum.'). How can these essentially meaningless monosyllables convey quite subtle responses? Maybe it's because the surprise implicit in the 'ho' is immediately undercut by the doubtfulness of **hum**. And consider 'um' and 'er', frequently coupled as a pair of dithering verbs: 'He ummed and erred but finally came round to my point of view.' 'Er' can crop up in uneasy introductions: 'And this lady is Mrs — Er?' And during the last few years it has achieved an odd status denied to other interjections, used regularly in print as a kind of rhetorical device, the equivalent of 'who'd have thought it?' The practice of using 'er' to signify something other than doubt or pure hesitation seems to have started with the satirical magazine *Private Eye*. At any rate, 'er's are frequently to be found in its pages, as in: 'She has sold her television production company, Shine, for 415m to, er, Daddy.' The magazine's deployment of 'er' is almost always ironic. It hints at double standards or hypocrisy. It says that what follows may seem to be surprising but isn't, not really.

PECCADILLO

❦ (1600) ❧

THERE ARE TWO SEPARATE streams of words deriving from Spain that have entered the English language. One, arguably the dominant word stream, has enjoyed a roundabout journey, either crossing the Atlantic with the early Spanish conquerors, missionaries and settlers to establish itself in the Americas before looping back across the ocean to find a home in British English, or alternatively deriving from altogether non-European sources since many words were brought back from Central American languages by those same Spanish imperialists. (See entry for **Barbecue**, one out of a substantial number of such expressions, page 187.) The other word stream has had a shorter journey, arriving more or less directly from Spain. It's not always easy to separate the two, but most of the expressions given below are in this second category.

A **peccadillo** is defined on its first recorded appearance in 1600 as a 'minor sin', a 'little fault', by the Dean of Exeter. There was a similar word in Italian, and both come ultimately from Latin sin-related words (*peccare*: 'to sin'). **Peccadillo** never seems to have been applied in real condemnation, and it's now used, generally in the plural form, with indulgence and even a touch of fondness: after all, where would most people be without their peccadilloes, peculiarities and idiosyncrasies? Another familiar Spanish-born term is 'aficionado', originally applied in the early nineteenth century to an amateur bullfighter before settling on its current sense of an enthusiastic, knowledgeable follower – but always an amateur, not a professional.

Apart from *matador* and perhaps *picador*, bullfighting terms have not made much impression on English. Yet the flamboyantly masculine spirit of the spectacle emerges in two significant terms. One of them is *macho* (Spanish: 'masculine') and the related *machismo* ('manliness'), both first cited in the US in the early 1940s. My impression is that, at least in British English, macho and machismo often appear tinged with scepticism and sometimes outright mockery. The second expression is *cojones* or testicles or, properly speaking, 'balls'. *Cojones* never conveys the characteristically British sense of rubbish/cobblers but has positive and manly connotations of 'nerve', 'coolness under fire'. *Cojones* are big in the USA on every level – George W. Bush was known to employ the term – because of the Hispanic influence on the language, but the word has spread to the UK, where it has also made its presence felt in the political arena. During a public meeting in 2014, Miriam González Durántez, the Spanish-born wife of the then Liberal Democrat leader Nick Clegg spoke out 'in favour of fathers who look after their children, saying they have "more cojones" […] Chuckling, the deputy prime minister told the audience of City fathers that he was grateful he did not need to translate the word *cojones*, adding: "Of course I agree with you. I always do."' (*Guardian*)

Spanish has given us a clutch of other disparate words, from *amontillado* (the sherry from Montilla in southern Spain) to *guerrilla*, sometimes *guerilla* (the diminutive of *guerra* [war], and so 'little war', and then applied to a fighter in such a war), to *patio* ('courtyard'). The oldest of such words (i.e. the first to surface in English) is probably *mosquito*, appearing in 1572 as *Muskito*. This is an example of a word that was picked up from the Spanish by other early voyagers to the Americas. Before then, the mosquito had been the Anglo-Saxon 'gnat' to the English. Another long-established Spanish import is the anchovy (Spanish: *anchoa*): Shakespeare has it with a slightly different spelling in *Henry IV, Part I* when part of Falstaff's bar bill is revealed to include 'Item anchaues and sacke* after supper. 2,s, vj,d' [2s.6d.]. Although they have been in English for a long time, terms such as *fiesta* ('festival', first referred to in English in 1844), *siesta* ('afternoon rest', deriving from Latin *sexta* or sixth [hour], first appearing 1655) and *plaza* ('public square'; 1683) have doubtless grown more familiar because of the popularity of Spain as a holiday destination among the British. Less well-known is the origin of *vanilla* (both the pod and the flavouring produced from it), since the word is ultimately related to the Latin *vagina* or sheath, and begins to appear in English in various spellings in the second half of the seventeenth century. This 'pod' definition has nothing to do with the recent identification of 'vanilla' with bland, conventional sex, which seems to have arisen as a piece of gay vernacular in the early 1970s, and reflects the idea that the vanilla flavour in ice-creams is the safe, predictable choice.

---

* Sack was a popular wine imported from Spain, though the name probably derives from French *vin sec* ('dry wine'). Falstaff's taste for sack is a running joke in *Henry IV, Part I*; the word appears 23 times in the play.

COFFEE

≈ (1601) ≈

THERE'S A STORY THAT when **coffee** first reached Rome late in the sixteenth century, certain priests tried to have it banned or excommunicated from Christendom because it was a 'hellish brew' which had come from lands to the east. Pope Clement VIII, made curious by all the fuss, decided to try this satanic substance. A sip or two was enough to convince him that it would be a shame to let the non-believers have exclusive use of this new drink: 'We shall fool Satan by baptising it and making it a truly Christian beverage.'

Perhaps the only verifiable thing about this story is that **coffee** did indeed reach Europe out of the east, and not just the drink but the word too. It comes via Turkish, where it was pronounced *kahveh*, from the Arabic *qahwah*, a term of uncertain meaning. The similarity of the word across the major European languages (*Kaffee, koffie, café, caffè*) indicates a common word root. There are plenty of English variant spellings to be found in **coffee**'s early years – *cahve, cohu, coffa, caffa* – but the spelling was soon normalized and the drink quickly caught on, even if it was a sometimes contentious habit. J. S. Bach didn't only produce exalted religious music; in the 1730s he also wrote a piece known as the Coffee Cantata (*Kaffeekantate*) about a girl whose addiction to the drink causes ructions with her father. The first written reference to a coffee house in England is to one in Oxford around 1650 and during the next century coffee houses and chocolate houses proliferated, particularly in London. Lloyd's, the insurers, started in Edward Lloyd's coffee house, since it was a place frequented by shipping merchants. During the nineteenth century the term 'café' gradually eased aside the coffee house.

Coffee is always hip, it seems, and never more so than at a time when the chain coffee shops act like big corporations while pretending not to be anything of the sort, and the indie, artisan outfits have an almost fetishistic appeal. The business has thrown up a host of new expressions to describe ever more niche products from *affogato* to *americano* to *mocha* to *macchiato*. This is a good example of the gloss that non-English words, particularly Italian ones, can give to regular items of food or drink, since *affogato* is Italian for 'drowned' while *macchiato* means 'stained'. *Mocha*, from the Yemeni port of that name, has a much older pedigree. The most pretentious term is surely *barista*, originally meaning 'barman' in Italian, in which language it may carry more weight. According to the journalist and writer Paul Hofmann, author of *Rome: The Sweet Tempestuous Life* (1982) and the apparent importer of the term into English, the expert behind the bar is apparently able to do three things at once: 'keep an eye on the coffee oozing from the espresso machine...pour vermouth and bitters...and discuss the miserable showing of the Lazio soccer team.' But that was in Rome and described the situation more than thirty years ago. Perhaps it's still like that today. In England, however, a *barista* is the person who makes you a cup of coffee which you pay for. That's all.

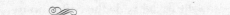

MULTITUDINOUS

❧ (1603) ❧

I N SHAKESPEARE'S PLAY *MACBETH*, the first murder
committed by the title character is that of Duncan,
the king of Scotland. Macbeth murders because
he is prompted to it by the predictions of the three
witches ('All hail, Macbeth, that shalt be king hereafter!'),
by the urging of his wife, and by his own ambition for
the throne.

He is no stranger to killing on the battlefield, but killing the king, when Duncan is an honoured guest in his
own castle of Dunsinane, is an entirely different business. As he emerges from the king's bedchamber after the
deed and stands in the courtyard, he gazes with horror at
his bloodstained hands. It's as if they don't belong to him
any longer.

What hands are here? Hah! They pluck out mine eyes.
Will all great Neptune's ocean wash this blood
Clean from my hand? No; this my hand will rather
The multitudinous seas incarnadine,
Making the green one red.

It's a brilliant dramatic moment. Only the appearance of Lady Macbeth shakes him out of his state of appalled introspection, when she tells him to clean himself up and put his nightgown on in case anyone wonders why he's still up and dressed long after midnight. But it's also a brilliant linguistic moment. Macbeth's sense of guilt is overwhelming: he imagines that his bloody hand will turn the sea red, rather than being cleansed by it. I seem to remember Ian McKellen, when he was playing Macbeth for the Royal Shakespeare Company in the 1970s, making a wave-like motion with his hand when he spoke the line: 'The multitudinous seas incarnadine'. The long-and-short syllables in the words have the choppiness of the sea.

Multitudinous (massed and plentiful) makes its initial appearance in English in 1603. *Macbeth* was first performed three years later, in 1606, so Shakespeare was among the earliest users of the word. 'Multitude', the source of **multitudinous**, goes back to the fourteenth century. The word comes from Latin (*multus*: 'much') via Norman French. One of the signs of its Latin/French origin is that it is a long, not to say complicated, word of five syllables. Compare it with the single-syllable 'much', deriving from the Old English *mickle*. It is a consistent feature of the English language that the great majority of the terms that come from Old English are shorter and simpler than the ones that came across in the wake of the Norman Conquest. In the final line that Macbeth speaks before his wife appears – 'Making the green one red' – every single word derives from Old English.

And what about *incarnadine*? It's an adjective meaning flesh-coloured, bright pink, and one of a group of words related to flesh or one of its colours that ultimately derive from Latin (incarnate, carnage, carnation). Shakespeare was the first person to use *incarnadine* as a verb rather than an adjective. So at the end of Macbeth's heartfelt speech there is one line consisting of two long 'new' words separated by an Old English word (sea), and then another line which is a kind of translation of the previous one, rendered in short sharp monosyllables. This is a living example of the two great streams that make up the great part of the English we use today: words from over a thousand years ago alongside words which come to us via French and Latin, trickling in over the centuries after the arrival of the Normans in 1066.

DISASTER

≈ (1604) ≈

EVERY AGE IS SUPERSTITIOUS after its own fashion but some are more superstitious than others. Elizabethan England paid greater attention to planetary influences, horoscopes and star signs than we do today, and the ideas behind such things, half-scientific, half-magical, were taken more seriously. Shakespeare's plays contain around 150 references to stars, comets and planets, the majority of which stress their potential to influence human affairs, usually for the worse. **Disaster** is intimately related to the idea of bad luck or trouble arising from some malign and distant source since the word, deriving from the French *désastre*, couples the negative prefix dis- to the word for 'star' (French: *aster*; Latin: *astrum*). 'Star' in this context could also apply to one of the planets, since no very clear distinction seems to have been made between the planetary bodies in the solar system and the stellar ones far beyond – a trace of which usage survives in references to Venus as the 'evening star'.

Shakespeare was the first person to use **disaster** as a noun in its modern sense of 'calamity', 'great personal misfortune'. In fact, he uncouples the word from its source-meaning when he has the villainous Edmund in *King Lear* (1604) contemptuously reject the idea that the stars control our fortunes. Like other strong characters such as Iago (*Othello*) or Cassius (*Julius Caesar*), Edmund insists that we are responsible for what happens to us, even as we try to wriggle out of the responsibility when we 'make guilty of our disasters, the sun, the moon, and the stars'. It's impossible to know what, if anything, Shakespeare himself believed about the influence of the planets or stars. He puts fatalistic words into the mouths of good characters and defiant ones into the mouths of bad characters. But the notion of being 'ill-starred' or – like the lovers Romeo and Juliet – 'star-crossed' and so bound for **disaster** is central to his plays.

Shakespeare is sometimes spoken of as if he made up dozens, if not hundreds, of completely new words in English. It's true that he did create a fair number by adapting words or combining elements of words which already existed: *bubuckles* to describe blotches on the face, a combination of 'bubo' (the swelling often associated with the plague) and 'carbuncle', *rooky* for a sinister evocation of dusk in *Macbeth* ('Light thickens,/And the crow makes wing to the rooky wood'), *intrenchant*, again from *Macbeth*, and describing the air which can't be cut by a sword blade, *immoment* to mean 'insignificant' (of no moment), and 'eventful'. But it would be more accurate to say that Shakespeare put pre-existing words to new uses. Examples include *palmy* in the sense of 'flourishing', 'successful' ('In the most high and palmy state of Rome'), *incarnadine* (see **multitudinous** above, page 137) and *seamy* in the sense of 'crude' or 'distasteful', because garments turned inside out have the seams showing and so feel rough to the touch. In some cases, it isn't always clear whether Shakespeare actually created a new word or whether it was already current and he just happened to be the first recorded user in English, as with **disaster** above. Among many other such examples are: inauspicious, hurry, assassination, accommodation (in the sense of providing room and food), countless, gloomy and critic.

Not all of Shakespeare's coinages and adaptations have lasted. If they appear in dictionaries at all it is because *he* wrote them rather than some other and now forgotten playwright scribbling away in a candlelit garret in Southwark. Among Shakespeare's coinages and adaptations which have not made the linguistic cut are: *disponge* ('to discharge from a squeezed sponge'), *congreet* ('to greet mutually'), *attasked* ('taken to task') and *convive* ('feast together'). The key feature to Shakespeare's contribution to English, however, lies less in the words that he created, adapted or tweaked than in his linguistic daring, his fluidity and sweep. He made words work. He encouraged them to jump through new hoops, for example by turning nouns into verbs as in 'out-Herods Herod'* from *Hamlet*, or adjectives into verbs: 'Thank me no thankings, nor proud me no prouds,' says father Capulet to his daughter in *Romeo and Juliet* (see also **Cabin**, page 67). Another father lecturing his daughter – Prospero to Miranda in *The Tempest* – throws out the phrase 'the dark backward and abysm of time', casually transforming an adverb (backward) into a noun as he talks about the remote past.

Perhaps even more striking than individual words is the substantial number of phrases that Shakespeare introduced and which have been part of the language ever since. Jealousy is 'green-eyed' because that's how Portia refers to it in *The Merchant of Venice*, the same play which

---

* 'It out-herods Herod: pray you, avoid it.' Hamlet is instructing the players who are visiting Elsinore in how to act the play which he believes will confirm his uncle Claudius's guilt in the murder of his father. King Herod of Judea was a byword for cruelty, because he commanded the massacre of the innocents after the birth of Christ. But the reference isn't so much to Herod's ruthlessness as to the crude, over-the-top style in which the king was depicted in the medieval Mystery plays. Hamlet is saying to the actors, in effect, be subtle, don't ham it up.

gives us 'blinking idiot'; Falstaff justifies playing dead on a battlefield by claiming that 'the better part of valour is discretion'; King Lear describes himself as 'more sinned against than sinning'; Antony accuses Cleopatra of playing 'fast and loose' with him (the reference is to a street con-game) while Cleopatra refers to her youth as her 'salad days'. In *Richard III*, Lord Hastings, condemned by Richard, is told: 'Make a short shrift; he longs to see your head.' The reference is to a brief space of time allowed to a criminal to make his confession (shrift) before execution; now to 'give short shrift' is to 'make quick work of' or 'brush aside'. And so on, and on and on with the Shakespearean phrases, to the 'crack of doom' (from *Macbeth*).

REBUS

❧ (1605) ❧

ARLY IN 2016 THERE was a row over the bronze
statue of a cock* in Jesus College, Cambridge. It
was one of hundreds of artefacts stolen from the
Benin empire (now part of Nigeria) after a punitive British naval expedition that destroyed the African kingdom
in 1897. The bronze bird was bequeathed to the college by
a British army officer, because cocks are a college emblem
and appear on its coat of arms. And the reason the cocks are

---

* The cock caused problems for the media in reporting on the Jesus College story.
The statue was generally referred to as a cockerel ('young cock'), while one paper
used the American-style 'rooster' in a headline. 'Cock' in general provokes uneasiness in English speakers because it has been slang for the penis since at least
the early seventeenth century. Linguistic delicacy is the reason why the 'hay-
stack' has driven out the 'haycock', or why the 'weathervane' is preferred to the
'weathercock'.

there in the first place is because Jesus College was founded in the fifteenth century by John Alcock, the bishop of Ely. The heraldic cocks are a visual allusion to his name, or a **rebus**. In St Bartholomew's Church in Smithfield there is another example of the **rebus**: a diamond-shaped stained glass depicting an arrow piercing a barrel, a visual pun on the name of the long-gone Prior Bolton ('bolt' + 'tun') of St Bartholomew's. A **rebus**, then, is a puzzle in which a word or phrase is cryptically represented by images or symbols. It may involve numbers and letters. There used to be a sign displayed in some pubs that looked a bit like a car licence plate and took this form: RU/18 or 1/8? In other words: are you over 18 or one over the eight?

The term was first used in English by the historian and antiquarian William Camden (1551–1623) in his *Remaines of a Greater Worke, Concerning Britaine* (1605), usually known simply as *Remaines*, a title which shows a certain candour about what to call a rag-bag collection of essays. Camden explains how French fashions had always influenced the English and especially so since the time of Edward III and his planting of colonies in northern France, bordering on the Picardy region. The Picards had a taste for making visual puns on their names, as Camden explains:

> whereas a Poesie is a speaking picture, and a picture a speechless Poesie, they which lack'd wit to express their conceit

['imaginative idea'] in speech did use to depaint it out (as it were) in pictures, which they called Rebus, by a Latine name well fitting their device. These were so well liked by our English there, and, sent over the streight of Calice [Calais] with full sail, were so entertained here (although they were most ridiculous) by all degrees, by the learned and unlearned, that he was no body that could not hammer out of his name an invention by this wit-craft.

Among several other examples, Camden describes how the Abbot of Ramsey in Cambridgeshire used as his seal the image of a ram in the sea.

As cryptic as the thing itself is the origin of the word. **Rebus** is the ablative plural of the Latin *res* ('thing') and means 'by things', so it is probable that the reference is to some longer phrase suggesting a puzzle to be solved not through the interpretation of words but 'by things'. A less likely source is the French word *rebours* which in the phrase *à rebours* signifies things done backwards or the wrong way round. The name of Ian Rankin's troubled hero, John Rebus, suggests his detective's skill at deciphering riddles, unpicking puzzles (Rankin's first book was titled *Knots and Crosses*).

DELPHIAN

~ (1625) ~

REFERENCES IN THE PLAYS of Shakespeare and his contemporaries, as well as in poetry of earlier periods, show that knowledge of the classical world was widespread, and that even the 'groundlings'* of the Elizabethan theatre would be expected to pick up what was meant. The landscape of Greece provided names evocative of a distant, mythical place and era. In Shakespeare's *The Winter's Tale* (1610) King Leontes sends two of his courtiers to Delphi, the oracular shrine in central Greece where the priests of the god Apollo interpreted

---

* The 'groundlings' stood in the ground or pit of the theatre. These were the cheapest places and so probably the ones occupied by the least educated and discriminating members of the audience. Shakespeare is the first recorded user of this disparaging term, in *Hamlet* (first performed *c.*1601).

the utterances of a priestess seated on a tripod in a state of 'divine ecstasy'. If the priests were asked about matters of law and religion they were able to give straightforward answers, but when questioned about the future they grew more hazy and evasive. After all, the oracle wouldn't be an oracle if it didn't speak in *ainigmata*, the Greek word for riddles and the source of our enigmas. Appropriately, the adjectives **Delphian** (first cited in 1625) or Delphic (1599) are ambiguous too. Indeed the first appearance of **Delphian** is in a book about the dubious value of urine for diagnosing 'all diseases'.

Moving nearly 200 miles north of Delphi we reach Mount Olympus, the highest peak in Greece and the traditional home of the gods, and so the source of everything which is 'olympian' or god-like, lofty and aloof, and a word first appearing in English towards the end of the fifteenth century. This shouldn't be confused with 'Olympic' (as in the Games), named after a plain in Elis in southern Greece where the first Olympic Games were held during the eighth century BC. To the southeast of Elis lies Sparta, the capital of the ancient state of Laconia. Sparta attached more significance to military hardihood than the other Greek city-states and had a reputation for efficient action and unadorned speech ('laconic' comes from Laconia). Spartan is synonymous with 'tough' or 'rigorous', and was used in this sense from the middle of the seventeenth century. Also deriving from a real classical place is the modern sense of Marathon, used when capitalized to describe a long race (because a runner is supposed to have covered the twenty-two miles from Marathon to Athens with news of a victory over the Persians, though he fell down dead when he arrived). The word was a surprisingly late entrant into English, not used to describe an extended run until the beginning of the twentieth century. In lower-case spelling, marathon applies to any drawn-out and probably arduous event, while the -athon suffix sometimes appears in new expressions like 'talkathon' or 'telethon'.

Finally passing on, or passing over, you might find yourself crossing the Styx, one of the rivers that formed the boundary between this world and the underworld or Hades (the realm of departed spirits). Once applying to oaths which were inviolable, because the gods themselves feared to break an oath invoking the Styx, Stygian first appeared (in the spelling *stygion*) in English in a 1566 translation from the Latin author Seneca. From connoting something infernal, stygian then became merely murky as in 'stygian depths'. If you were unlucky, you ended up in the lowest of the infernal regions or Tartarus, a place of darkness and torment and, as a direct transliteration from Greek and Latin, first cited in English in 1586. If you were one of the fortunate, by contrast, you spent your after-life swanning around the Fields of Elysium (from a Greek expression for 'abode of the blessed'), an experience which can still be enjoyed by anyone visiting Paris and strolling down the Avenue des Champs-Élysées.

❧

MERETRICIOUS

∾ (1626) ∾

MERETRICIOUS NOW MEANS 'FLASHY', 'superficially attractive but without real worth'. ('Confronted with this gaudy and meretricious bauble, the prospective visitor may well turn away in despondency.' *The Spectator*) The word derives from a Latin word for 'prostitute', and it's in this context that it is first used in English, with the philosopher Francis Bacon referring to 'Meretricious Embracements' which 'maketh Marriage a dull thing'. The word has wandered away from its sexual context though it still tends to be used about an alluring appearance, though of things not people, as well as applying to attractive-seeming ideas, proposals, etc. Both 'prostitute', first noted in English in a noun sense in 1607 though it was earlier used as a verb as well as an adjective (in the sense of 'debased', 'corrupt'), and 'fornication' also derive from Latin. This word, first cited in a Middle English religious poem written some time before 1300 and denoting one of the branches of the sin of lechery (specifically, non-marital sex), has a curious and contested etymology. *Fornix* is Latin for an 'arch' or 'vault', and the connection with sex seems to be that it was in such sheltered places that the prostitutes would wait for their clients. Fornication can be used in English to mean 'arching' in the architectural sense; for understandable reasons such references are very limited.

CLUE

❦ (?1630s) ❦

I N 'THE FINAL PROBLEM' (1893), the short story which Arthur Conan Doyle wrote to kill off Sherlock Holmes, the great detective is on the trail of the man who is intended to be his nemesis, Professor Moriarty. Telling Watson that he has spent a long time in pursuit of 'some deep organising power' that is behind a variety of crimes from forgery to murder, Holmes says: 'For years I have endeavored to break through the veil which shrouded it [the organising power], and at last the time came when I seized my thread and followed it, until it led me, after a thousand cunning windings, to ex-Professor Moriarty of mathematical celebrity.'

Holmes's image of seizing a thread and following it through a maze to arrive at a happy outcome (or a solution) goes back to the Greek myth of Theseus and the Minotaur. Before Theseus enters the labyrinth, at the heart of which lurks the monster who is half-man, half-bull, he is given a sword and a ball of string by Ariadne, daughter of King Minos. Theseus uses the sword to kill the Minotaur and the thread from the unwound ball to retrace his steps out of the labyrinth. Such a ball of thread or yarn was once called a *clew* (found in different spellings in the tenth and eleventh centuries) and derived from Old English *cliwen*, signifying a round object composed of coiled-up material. From there it's a short step to **clue**, first used in its modern sense and spelling in the first half of the seventeenth century by the courtier and adventurer Kenelm Digby (the dating is uncertain because the word occurs in the preface to a journal he kept of a Mediterranean voyage, unpublished until the nineteenth century).

Sherlock Holmes, by following clues (or *clews*) to the heart of the labyrinth, finds his own Minotaur in Moriarty, whom he compares to 'a spider in the centre of its web'. And, like Theseus, Holmes survives the encounter with his personal monster. Despite Doyle's original plan of finishing with his burdensome hero in 'The Final Problem', a mixture of public demand and financial inducement brought Holmes back to life nearly ten years later in *The Hound of the Baskervilles* (1902).

JUGGERNAUT

≈ (1638) ≈

O DORIC OF PORDENONE WAS a Franciscan friar who combined missionary work and exploration in the East during the early fourteenth century, later writing an account of his travels. In eastern India he witnessed a religious procession that involved self-sacrifice on a mass scale. In the words of a nineteenth-century translation of *Cathay and the Way Thither*, this is what Odoric saw:

> …annually on the recurrence of the day when that idol was
> made, the folk of the country come and take it down, and
> put it on a fine chariot; and then the king and queen, and all
> the pilgrims, and the whole body of the people, join together
> and draw it forth from the church with loud singing of songs

and all kinds of music [...] And many pilgrims who have come to this feast cast themselves under the chariot, so that its wheels may go over them, saying that they desire to die for their God. And the car passes over them, and crushes and cuts them in sunder, and so they perish on the spot [...] And thus not a year passes but there perish more than five hundred men in this manner; and their bodies they burn, declaring that they are holy, having thus devoted themselves to death for their God.

The Hindu festival which the Franciscan friar observed involved the god/idol *Jagannath* (Sanskrit: 'lord of the world'). It would be around 300 years after Odoric's time before the word **juggernaut** entered the English language (in the spelling *Iagarnat* in 1638) but the ceremony continued to involve a voluntary mass sacrifice by pilgrims until at least the end of the eighteenth century. To call the shrine containing the **juggernaut** a car or chariot scarcely does it justice; Indian images from the Victorian era show something like a cross between a siege-machine, an armoured car and a temple on wheels. It is in this sense – i.e. as a very large, heavy vehicle – that the word tends to be used now, as it has been since the 1970s when there was much environmental concern about juggernauts thundering through thatched and Tudor-beamed villages. The word also has a thriving metaphorical life to denote some supposedly unstoppable force which is going to crush everyone in its path ('Trump juggernaut is poised to capture 10 of the next 14 primary states…' *Daily Mail*). In this latter sense, **juggernaut** may also contain the idea of a 'bandwagon'.

❧

BATHOS

≈ (1638) ≈

THE WORD **BATHOS** FIRST appears in 1638 in a published sermon by Robert Sanderson, Bishop of Lincoln. He is talking of God's love and says there is 'such a βάθος in every dimension of it'. Sanderson used the Greek word in its original Greek form, one which would have been familiar to an educated readership. He also used it approvingly with the sense of 'depth', a sense that survives in words such as 'bathyscaphe' (usually appearing as 'bathyscape') and 'bathysphere' describing a deep-sea exploration craft. But by the eighteenth century **bathos** has undergone its own kind of descent from a term implying profundity to one which indicates a crashing lurch from the grand to the trivial, a different kind of drop to the bottom: a come-down, an anticlimax.

It's been claimed that the British are masters of the art, as suggested by this observation from the *Guardian*: 'The diarist's default mode is bathos. "As I reluctantly swung out of bed I noticed my feet," wrote Alec Guinness on the first day of 1995, "never something on which I like to dwell."'

As a term **bathos** applies to some literary or rhetorical effects that may be unintended* but are sometimes deliberately engineered, especially in comedy. To judge such things, whether as writer or reader, one may need the help of another Greek term: 'criterion' (plural 'criteria') or a test or standard of judgement. Like **bathos**, criterion was often written in its original Greek form of κριτήριον following its first appearance in English in 1647. **Bathos** is one of a clutch of specialist expressions in the English language deriving directly from Greek, both in form and meaning and all relating to various tricks and turns of expression, whether in speech or on the page. These range from *aposiopesis* to *zeugma*, via *litotes* and *tmesis* and many others. It is no accident that these Greek-derived words should

---

* One of the most famous examples of literary bathos occurs in William Wordsworth's poem 'The Thorn', an authentically tragic ballad involving illegitimacy, death and wintery uplands. In the third verse Wordsworth literally gets out his measuring tape – this is not a joke – and the whole episode rises, or rather sinks, to an anticlimax: 'Not five yards from the mountain-path,/This thorn you on your left espy;/And to the left, three yards beyond,/You see a little muddy pond/Of water, never dry,/I've measured it from side to side:/'Tis three feet long, and two feet wide.' Wordsworth later changed the final couplet to read 'Though but of compass small, and bare/To thirsty suns and parching air.'

be added to the English lexicon in what is, historically speaking, the early modern period, for this was an age that saw a rapid expansion of knowledge in science and medicine, and an appreciation of the classical roots of the new, humanist world.

Rhetorical terms like those mentioned above may sound unfamiliar but what they describe is not. *Aposiopesis* or 'becoming silent', first noted in English in 1578, is a deliberate breaking-off of speech as in 'What the— ?'* Anyone using the very English response of 'Not bad' to a question like 'What did you think of the film?' is employing *litotes* (1656) or understatement. *Tmesis* (1592), from the Greek for cutting, occurs when a word (usually a swear-word) is shoved into another word: abso-bloody-lutely! *Zeugma*, in Greek signifying 'yoking' and first cited in 1589, is a figure of speech where a single word is made to apply to a pair of other words in a context where it would more usually apply to one. A well-known example occurs in Charles Dickens's *Pickwick Papers*: 'Miss Bolo rose from the table considerably agitated, and went straight home, in a flood of tears and a sedan-chair.' For another example, see what happens with the verb 'bounce' in this sentence from

---

* A fine illustration of aposiopesis comes at the very end of Laurence's Sterne's novel *A Sentimental Journey Through France and Italy* (1765). The last sentence reads: 'So that when I stretch'd out my hand, I caught hold of the Fille de Chambre's—.'

The Times: 'The company's [Google] large office in Covent Garden...features a secret garden with allotments, acoustic airlocks and even a padded cell for those meetings where you want to bounce people, as well as ideas, around.' Bouncing people and ideas around is pure zeugma.

TELESCOPE

⁓ (1648) ⁓

WHEN JOHN MILTON (1608-74) was travelling in Italy as a young man, he went to Florence where he 'found and visited the famous Galileo, grown old, a prisoner to the Inquisition, for thinking in astronomy otherwise than the Franciscan and Dominican licensers thought'. Many years later, while composing his monumental work *Paradise Lost*, the poet paid tribute to Galileo and the 'optic glass' through which the astronomer gazed at the moon 'to descry [make out] new lands, / Rivers or mountains in her spotty globe.' Milton, like Galileo, was excited by the idea of new worlds and planets.* Galileo

---

* John Milton coined the word 'Pandemonium' in *Paradise Lost* for the place where the devils gather in hell to plan their revenge against God, who has driven them by force from heaven. The great edifice that the devils construct, half palace, half

used the Italian word *telescopio* in his letters, a new expression for a new thing in early seventeenth-century Italy. The term, which arrived in English a little later, results from combining two Greek words meaning 'far off' and 'look'. By a neat symmetry, the same year (1648) also sees the first citation in English for 'microscope', which, like its big brother **telescope**, comes to us from Greek via Italian (*microscopio*).

The seventeenth century was an age of experiment and advance. As new facets of the world opened up, new words were needed both to describe the discoveries and also the instruments and equipment which enabled those discoveries in the first place. As was usual in scientific circles then and since, Latin and Greek were looked to as linguistic treasure troves. The discoverers/inventors were steeped in the classics, and Latin was the language in which scholarly and scientific treatises were generally published. The 'barometer' was invented in 1643, and the word formed from two Greek terms meaning 'weight' and 'measure'. Galileo explored the scientific properties of the 'pendulum' while Latin provided the word (from *pendeo*: 'hang down'); it was a Dutch scientist who designed the first

---

city, combines two Greek words (*pan*: 'all' + *daimon*: 'spirit'). *Pandemonium* was first a 'centre of wickedness' and then simply a 'scene full of noise and confusion'. Ironically, the original Pandemonium in Milton's version is grand, well-ordered and relatively tranquil, a place for debate rather than fighting.

pendulum clock in 1657. The energetic Galileo was also the first to create an elementary 'thermometer', a word from Greek sources which first appeared in French as *thermomètre* before arriving in English in 1633.

Apart from instruments like the 'microscope' used in discovery, there was also the task of naming the things that had been found. William Harvey's 1628 treatise on the principles of blood-circulation called *De Motu Cordis* (the full title translated from the Latin *Exercitatio Anatomica de Motu Cordis et Sanguinis in Animalibus* is 'An Anatomical Exercise on the Motion of the Heart and Blood in Living Beings') eventually spread the notion of 'circulation', another Latin borrowing, from animals to the movement of sap in plants, and later to the free movement of anything from newspapers to currency to traffic. The mid-seventeenth century also saw the earliest application of 'corpuscle' to a 'minute body' (diminutive of Latin: *corpus*) and the first accurate description of the oxygen-bearing red corpuscles in the bloodstream. 'Gas' was modelled on the Greek word 'chaos' and, somewhat surprisingly, the word is attributable to an individual, the Flemish scientist Jan Baptist van Helmont. 'Atmosphere' (Greek: 'vapour' + 'ball/sphere') is another example of a new word, first describing the 'gaseous envelope' around a heavenly body and then acquiring its metaphorical sense of the 'predominant mood' of a place in the late eighteenth century.

Both of the next words are seventeenth-century Latin borrowings: 'refraction' describing the way in which rays of light bend as they pass from one medium to another, and 'spectrum' (originally with the sense of 'apparition' or 'spectre') characterizing the splitting-up of light into a band of colours. The 'prism', which breaks up the beam of light, has a strange derivation since it comes from the Greek for 'to saw', and means 'a piece (of wood) sawn off' in allusion to the shape and solidity of the device.

This crucial scientific century sees the creation of new words, usually from Latin and Greek, paralleling the invention of new things, or the re-tooling of older terms so that they are given a new scientific purpose. 'Gravity' meant metaphorical 'weight' or 'seriousness' before the term took on its scientific and physical application to describe the downward tendency of things or the influence of one planetary body on another. Similarly, 'attraction', used of magnets and lodestones since the reign of Elizabeth I, takes on its astronomical meaning in the writings of Isaac Newton later in the following century. You could say that such old terms are provided with a new 'focus', another seventeenth-century Latin borrowing with the meaning of 'hearth' or 'fireplace' and probably used scientifically because it was appropriate for the combustible meeting point of the beams or rays which streamed through a lens or 'burning glass'.

QUARANTINE

∼ (1649) ∼

THERE ARE TWO MEN called Lazarus in the Bible. One is the Lazarus whom Jesus raises from the dead (John: 11); the other is Lazarus the beggar, who appears in a parable (Luke: 16) sitting by the rich man's gate while the dogs lick his sores and the rich man (occasionally called *Dives*: 'rich', Latin) passes him by. In the Middle Ages, the poor man gave his name to the *lazar*, a wretched and diseased individual, sometimes identified as a leper. Those afflicted by the disease might be confined in a lazar-house or, in Italian, a *lazaretto*. The word could apply not just to a house but to an entire island, the safest place to isolate sufferers from leprosy as well as suspected plague-carriers, and it was the Venetian Republic that in 1423 established the first such place on one of the islands in the Venetian Lagoon. It set a precedent. Victoria Hislop's bestseller *The Island* (2005) is based on Spinalonga, a *lazaretto* just off the Cretan seaside resort of Elounda and still a slightly unsettling place to be when the sun begins to go down and you wait for the last ferry of the day to carry you back the few hundred yards to the mainland.

There are other similar sites in Europe, traces of which remain. The *lazarettos* and *lazarets* were not constructed only for the poor and sick, but to keep returning healthy travellers in isolation until time proved they were not disease-carriers. Byron stayed at the Maltese *lazaretto* in Valletta on his way back from cholera-ridden Greece in 1811. There is a quai Lazaret in Marseilles, the locale for the opening of Charles Dickens's novel *Little Dorrit* (1857), where barrack buildings were used to isolate travellers returning from the east and possible contact with the plague. The original island *lazaretto* is referenced in Ben Jonson's black comedy *Volpone* (1607) set in Venice 'Where they [ships] use to lie out forty, fifty days, sometimes, about the Lazaretto, for their trial.' The 'trial' was the forty-day period needed to establish whether a ship and its passengers arriving from 'any suspected part of all the Levant' were clean. The word **quarantine** already existed in English in varying spellings to describe a period of penance lasting forty days (as in Christ's time in the wilderness or the observation of Lent). The secular sense may derive from old Italian *quarantina*, since that is where the system started (Italian, *quaranta*: 'forty').

LEXICOGRAPHER

≈ (1658) ≈

L EXICOGRAPHER DERIVES FROM TWO ancient Greek words, with a meaning that approximates to 'a writer on words', and was first used in a seventeenth-century zoological book, as translated from Latin. (It was customary for scientific and other academic texts to be produced initially in Latin, the *lingua franca* of European scholars.) Samuel Johnson, the great English **lexicographer**, provided a half-ironic definition of his trade in his own *Dictionary of the English Language*, published in 1755: '*Lexicographer*, a writer of dictionaries; a harmless drudge, that busies himself in tracing the original, and detailing the signification of words.' The dominant figure in English literary and cultural life of the mid-eighteenth century, Dr Johnson (1709–84) produced the first dictionary of real weight and authority in English. Employing six assistants, five Scots and one English, who worked in the garret floor of his rented house off Fleet Street, and whose task was to copy out quotations to illustrate the words being defined, Johnson reserved the intellectual spade-work for himself alone. He not only selected, from his own vast reading, almost a quarter of a million illustrative quotations, of which around half were actually used, but he wrote the definitions to more than 40,000 words.

In one of those you-couldn't-make-it-up-if-you-tried coincidences the first American **lexicographer** – i.e. the first compiler to produce a dictionary specifically aimed at the American market – was Samuel Johnson Jr (1757–1836). Despite their twinned names, Dr Samuel Johnson, that dedicated Londoner, was in no way related to Samuel Johnson Jr, a life-long citizen of Guilford (Connecticut). But the **lexicographer** who really made his mark on a newly independent and increasingly confident America was Noah Webster with his two-volume *American Dictionary of the English Language* (1828). It was a very deliberate decision on Webster's part to depart from the standard English spelling of some words and so to Americanize them, as in 'caliber', 'plow', etc. (see also under **Fall**, p. 88), a practice which has been termed 'patriotic orthography'.

The days of the one-man-band general dictionary are long gone. The Scot James Murray (1837–1915) was the prime mover – the closest thing to a Johnson or a Webster – in the compilation of the *Oxford English Dictionary*, but the *OED*, arguably the most famous English language dictionary in the world, is the work of many lexicographical hands stretching not just over the decades but now over centuries. The idea for a truly compendious dictionary, to contain terms which have fallen out of use as well as giving a reliable history or etymology for every word included, first emerged in the 1850s. Initially issued in installments (A–Ant, etc.), in part for financial reasons, the full glory of *OED* would not be available in its ten-volume form until 1928.

Since a living language is never still, a dictionary's work can never be done. Accordingly, the *OED* was reissued in twelve volumes only five years after its first publication, with the addition of a one-volume Supplement. And, as the English language continually expands, around 1,000 new words a year are added to the online versions of the various Oxford dictionaries. This is as nothing compared to additions to what is known as the 'corpus', a vast array of lexical material whose expansion has really been facilitated by electronic retrieval and storage. According to the *OED* **lexicographer** Angus Stevenson, speaking in 2013: 'Each month, we add about 150 million words to our corpus database of English usage examples collected from sources around the world. We use this database to track and verify new and emerging words and senses on a daily basis.'

Despite Dr Johnson's ironic self-definition as a 'harmless drudge', lexicographical work not only illuminates our understanding of the depth, variety and flexibility of our own language but helps to trace out the links – cultural, social, historical, geographical and political – between all languages.

SHIBBOLETH

≈ (1658) ≈

I N NORTHERN IRELAND DURING the Troubles, the consequences of being told to read the sign above a well-known jewellers could be fatal. It was all down to the difference in the pronunciation of the letter 'h', with Catholics habitually saying 'haitch' and Protestants 'aitch'. In the attempt to find out which side someone was on, a paramilitary gunman might indicate the name above a shop and tell his potential victim to read it out. The shop in question? H. Samuel. This grim story has parallels throughout history, for a small difference in pronunciation or the inability to say a particular word can distinguish between friend and foe. At the end of the Second World War, Nazi spies and German soldiers fleeing Holland were detectable by their inability to utter the notoriously difficult names of the towns of Scheveningen and Nijmegen. A popular belief has German spies in Britain being tripped up by the word 'squirrel', since they would instinctively transform the 'q' into a 'kv' sound. Yet, as the writer and translator Peter Lewis points out in *The Word at War* (2014), it would hardly have been necessary for a suspicious Englishman to turn the conversation to squirrels* since the English phoneme 'th' – as in 'the' – is problematic not just for Germans but for other non-Anglophones as well.

These verbal hurdles are examples of a **shibboleth**, a word from Hebrew and meaning either an 'ear of corn' or, more probably, a 'stream in flood'. In the Old Testament book of Judges, the men of Gilead, who were fighting the men of Ephraim, employed **shibboleth** as a means of preventing the escape of the Ephraimites across the River Jordan. The men of Ephraim might have looked like the men of Gilead but they couldn't pronounce 'sh', saying 'sibboleth' instead. The era covered by the book of Judges dates back almost 3,000 years so it is likely that **shibboleth** is the oldest word in this twenty-first-century book. The term occurred earlier in English in biblical translations, but on its first non-biblical appearance in 1658, **shibboleth**

---

* By a curious reversal, there is evidence to suggest that the German word for 'squirrel', *Eichhörnchen*, was used to entrap spies or escaped POWs. The problem for an English speaker lies not only in the repeated 'ch' sound but also in the testing umlauted 'ö' in between.

signified a difficulty in pronunciation, and so a distinguishing feature of speech. Then, by extension, it comes to apply to other things like a style of dress or manner, which might mark out any group as being different. At some point in the twentieth century, the word takes on an additional sense, being applied to an old idea or set of beliefs which it would be bad taste, almost taboo, to question ('"Equal opportunities" is seen by some as a shibboleth of the politically-correct' *Daily Telegraph*). This strange word, surviving thousands of years from the time of the Old Testament, now has several related meanings but its connotations are faintly pejorative, with the 'unquestioned belief' sense taking precedence over the 'distinguishing mark' one.

The Old Testament has provided English with other Hebraic terms such as Babel, leviathan and messiah. In the Book of Genesis the descendants of Noah set about erecting a tower in Babel (a city in Babylonia, part of what is now Iraq) with the apparent aim of building bigger, higher and better than anyone else. But their upward aspirations merely provoked the wrath of God, who 'confound[ed] their language' and scattered the people 'abroad upon the face of the earth', so that after speaking one language they found themselves talking in many tongues. Everywhere was noise and misunderstanding, or a 'Babel'. Though the words overlap in their meaning, Babel is not etymologically related to 'babble', which probably comes from an onomatopoeic-style imitation of a child's early attempts at speech. There are Old English references to the Genesis story of the tower of Babel (in that spelling) while the use of the word, appearing as 'babell', to signify a confusion of sounds first occurs at the beginning of the 16th century. Leviathan was the Hebraic word for a giant aquatic beast ('Canst thou draw out leviathan with an hook? or his tongue with a cord which thou lettest down?' Job: 41, i), and first appears in the Wycliffe Bible, dated to 1382 or earlier; now the word is used for any large sea-going object from ship to whale, or pejoratively for a large organization of which the user disapproves. Messiah (in earlier versions such as the Wycliffe Bible spelled in the Greek style *messias*) comes from a Hebrew word meaning 'anointed' and does not appear to settle into its current form until the middle of the sixteenth century.

TERRIFIC

❧ (1667) ❧

JOHN MILTON'S EPIC POEM *Paradise Lost* (1667) tells the story of the expulsion of Adam and Eve from the Garden of Eden, their own paradise lost. Before the Fall, all of the animals in paradise were docile and harmless, even the snake who is destined to be the villain of the piece. Milton describes it as the 'subtlest beast of all the field,/Of huge extent sometimes, with brazen eyes/And hairy main terrific.' Leaving aside the poet's description of the snake's crest as hairy, we might wonder what he meant by **terrific**. Not 'impressive', though it probably was that, and certainly not 'excellent' as in the modern application of the word. Milton's **terrific** – the first time the word had been used in English – was much closer to the Latin root of *terrificus* ('terrifying'). About a century later, the word had slipped, or perhaps grown, to describe something 'of great size' or 'excessive' as it still does in, say, 'He made a terrific fuss.' By the late nineteenth century it becomes synonymous with 'splendid', 'fine'.

This process by which a word sheds its old meaning, rather like a snake shedding its skin, and takes on a new and arguably improved sense is known in the linguistic trade as 'amelioration.' So something **terrific** is now anything but terrifying. 'Pretty' was once the equivalent of modern 'crafty' (which used to mean skilful), while if you'd called someone 'nice' in the Middle Ages they might well have been offended since it suggested they were foolish, simple-minded. The opposite process, whereby a positive word takes on negative overtones, is called 'pejoration.' This is more usual than amelioration, probably on account of the old mud-sticking principle. It is hard for an expression to clean itself up, easy for it to get dirty. 'Awful' once meant 'inspiring awe and respect', while 'dreadful' indicated someone timid (i.e. full of dread). One of the early meanings of 'horrid' was 'bristling' (Latin: *horridus*). At one time 'egregious' suggested that the person or thing so described was known for their good qualities, while now it's their bad qualities. A curious example of pejoration concerns Walt Disney's best-known creation. Mickey Mouse made his cartoon debut in *Steamboat Willie* (1928). Within a few years the name of the mouse was being used to denote something small, insignificant, pointless.

BLOODY

❦ (1676) ❧

A TERRIBLE THING HAPPENED ON the first night of George Bernard Shaw's play *Pygmalion* in April 1914. The terrible thing lasted only a second, or even less, but it was enough to provoke near-hysteria in the audience at His Majesty's Theatre in London's Haymarket. So wild and uncontrolled was the laughter, wrote Shaw afterwards, 'that it was really doubtful for some time whether they could recover themselves and let the play go on.' That wasn't the end of the matter. As the notoriety of that split-second spread across the nation, bishops protested and called for the play to be banned. There were letters to *The Times*, angry newspaper articles on the subject, debates at Eton and the Oxford Union, and petitions to the prime minister.

And the source of all this to-do? It was a single word, which would pass almost unnoticed today, occurring in a play that is now better known in its film musical incarnation of *My Fair Lady*. In Shaw's *Pygmalion* Liza Doolittle is transformed by Professor Henry Higgins from a cockney flower-seller into someone who might be passed off as a duchess. Higgins, a professor of phonetics, takes on the task for a bet and to prove his (and Shaw's) ideas about the English, speech, pronunciation and class. Act III is set in Higgins's mother's flat on the Chelsea Embankment. It's her afternoon to receive visitors, and Higgins uses the occasion as a test for Liza. The trouble is that, as he explains to Mrs Higgins before the guests arrive, 'I've got her pronunciation all right, but you have to consider not only how a girl pronounces, but what she pronounces.' Liza arrives last and makes stilted conversation but the façade starts to crack, and finally when asked by a young man who's rather taken with her if she's walking back across the Park, Liza replies: 'Walk! Not bloody likely. [Sensation] I am going in a taxi.' Shaw, who paid almost as much attention to his stage directions as he did to his dialogue, inserted [Sensation] to show the effect of Liza's **bloody** on Mrs Higgins and her guests. But 'sensation' would be an understatement for the impact of the word on Edwardian England.

It took several centuries before **bloody**, coming from a Germanic word and initially appearing in Old English as *blodig*, took on the meaning which Shaw and Eliza Doolittle gave to it, and which so shocked his audience. The word applied literally to someone smeared in blood and metaphorically to someone with a taste for shedding it. More generally, **bloody** might characterize a battle or a particularly violent historical era. Then it's used in an apparently different sense in 1676 with a reference to being 'bloody drunk' in George Etherege's play *The Man of Mode*, although this might refer to the drinking habits of a young blood (i.e. a blotto aristo). **Bloody** doesn't definitively become the **bloody** we are familiar with until almost a hundred years later with references such as 'bloody bad news' and a 'bloody good song'. Here the word operates as an intensifier, in the same sense as 'absolutely' or 'extremely', but most often in a negative context. That is, hearing a piece of bloody *bad* news is more common, linguistically speaking, than hearing a bloody *good* song.

But why did the word make a leap from describing something matter-of-fact, if admittedly potentially unpleasant, to a term that was for many years almost taboo? The *OED* observes that for plenty of English speakers it was the strongest expletive available. All sorts of theories have been advanced, from its being a contracted form of *byrlady* (by our Lady), an old oath or interjection, to associations with menstrual blood or to Protestant suspicion of the Catholic belief in transubstantiation (the conversion of the red wine of communion into Christ's blood). In this respect it's worth noting the oaths of the Elizabethan age and earlier which invoked parts of Christ's body, including *'sblood* and *'swounds*. We'll most likely never know why **bloody** acquired such a dangerous reputation that it could not be uttered at the beginning of the twentieth century on a London stage without causing a hysteria similar to the response to Ken Tynan's first utterance of 'fuck' on a late-night BBC show in 1965 (see page 74). Underlying all the **bloody** business is probably an inherent uneasiness at the idea of blood and blood-letting. It may be the cumulative effect of a repeated coupling of the word with nouns like 'villain' and 'thief', so that **bloody** eventually came to combine ideas of badness and extremity.

SLOGAN

≈ (1680) ≈

I T MAY SEEM CURIOUS that **slogan**, a term irretrieva-
bly associated with brand-managers, spin-doctors
and advertisers, should go back as far as the seventeenth century, but it has even older roots. The word,
appearing earlier than 1680 in various forms such as
slogorne, sluggorn and *slughorn*, has the distinction of being
one of the few terms from Celtic or Gaelic to have survived
into modern English. Made up of two Gaelic words *sluagh*
and *ghairm* ('host' + 'shout'), the *slughorn* was the war-
cry of Highlanders or the native Irish, such a cry perhaps
consisting of a clan-name or a meeting-place. From the
nineteenth century the **slogan** begins to be applied first to
political and then to advertising campaigns, another word
with warlike overtones.

A handful of further words which seem to epitomize, respectively, Wales, Scotland and Ireland, at least from the visitor's point of view, have equally ancient roots. The 'bard' is particularly associated with Wales but is common to all three countries to describe a 'poet', and a term stretching back for the better part of two millennia since there is a reference by a late Roman historian to the *bardus* who sings the praises of heroes, a traditional role for the minstrel/versifier. 'Clan' comes from the Gaelic *clann*, but it is likely that its origin is actually the Latin *planta* ('shoot', 'scion'), with the p- being replaced by c-, and the derivation explicable by the fact that members of a clan claimed descent from a single person. 'Whisky' comes from, and is a shortened form of, the Gaelic *uisgebeatha*, which has the literal meaning 'water of life'. The one-letter difference between the spelling for Scotch, 'whisky', and the liquor distilled in Ireland and the US, 'whiskey', seems to be more a matter of branding than anything else. The *craic*, figuring in Irish tourist ads and used by the Irish themselves, may be seen as an essential to that country's culture with its sense of 'good company and conversation', probably accompanied with a Guinness or two. But far from being another ancient Gaelic term, *craic* is a recent import and an Irishification of *crack*, a Scottish and northern dialect term for 'brisk talk'.

In an amusing footnote to the history of **slogan**, the old spelling of *slughorn* caused Robert Browning to think that it was an archaic term for a war trumpet, which is how he mistakenly used it in his 1855 poem *Childe Roland to the Dark Tower Came*: 'Dauntless the slug-horn to my lips I set,/And blew.' The medieval setting of Browning's poem and the fact that slughorn had been similarly (mis)used earlier by the Bristol poet and forger of medieval documents, Thomas Chatterton, were responsible for Browning's blunder. This was hardly his worst linguistic slip, however. In his 1841 poem 'Pippa Passes', Browning was searching for a rhyme in a short list of ecclesiastical head-gear, and wrote: 'Then owls and bats,/cowls and twats,/Monks and nuns...' When Browning was asked many years later by the editors of the *Oxford English Dictionary* about his use of 'twat', he pointed them to a line from *Vanity of Vanities*, a seventeenth-century poem out of which he had extracted what he took to be an authentic item of cloistered head-gear: 'They talk't of his having a Cardinalls Hat,/They'd send him as soon an Old Nuns Twat.' It is not clear whether the *OED* editors ever revealed the true meaning of twat to Browning, or indeed whether they were aware of it themselves.

BARBECUE

≈ (1697) ≈

THE SPANISH CONTRIBUTION TO English comes from two sources. One is straight from that country (see **peccadillo**). But the more weighty linguistic cargo has undergone a longer journey, whether by spreading through North America and taking root there or by coming back across the Atlantic in the aftermath of imperial expansion in the New World. This quite significant area of English vocabulary in turn comes from two distinct sources: either from words that were indigenous to the Caribbean region and then assimilated into Spanish, or from words that were imported from Spain in the first place before returning to settle into English. The word 'cargo', as in the third sentence above, is an early example of such a Spanish export/import (first cited in English in 1657) and so are 'plaza' and 'tornado'. The most apparent Spanish legacy, though, is in US place names, which for obvious reasons predominate in the southwest of that country. The stamp of the language is literally everywhere, from the level of the states (Nevada: 'snow-covered') to the cities whether large (Los Angeles: 'the angels') or small (El Paso: 'the pass') to natural features (Rio Grande: 'big river').

The Caribe peoples who populated parts of the area which came under Spanish control not only gave their name to the Caribbean – the vast area once known as the Spanish Main – but, since some of them were reputed to eat human flesh, the word is also at the root of cannibal. 'Canoe' and 'hammock' are other examples which come to us, via Spanish, from Caribbean words. Perhaps the most surprising of these early indigenous/Spanish terms is **barbecue**. Far from being a twentieth-century term, the **barbecue** goes back a long way to the Spanish *barbacoa* which, in turn, was taken in the seventeenth century from a Haitian word describing a framework of sticks. Yet the earliest allusions in English to putting anything on a **barbecue** involve recumbent people rather than smoking meat, since the wooden framework served as a place to sleep. Another term associated with smoking and toasting is 'tobacco', derived from the Spanish *tabaco*, and ultimately from a Carib name for the dried leaves which were smoked by the indigenous inhabitants, or possibly for the tube or pipe used for inhaling the result. 'Potato' comes from Spanish *patata*, a variant on *batata*, a word of Haitian origin. From around the same period, 'tomato' and 'chocolate' were Spanish adaptations of *tomatl* and *chocolatl*, both terms from central America. And emerging slightly later, 'cocoa/cacao' comes from the Aztec *cacahuatl* while the 'avocado' is indebted to the Aztec *ahuacatl*. This grew on the *ahuacacuahatl* or 'testicle tree', named – obviously! – for the shape and droopiness of ripening avocados. In the US the avocado is sometimes called the 'alligator pear', a name that arose either from a mishearing of the indigenous name of the fruit or on account of its hard, bumpy skin, or both.

A number of terms which we regard as characteristic of the west and southwest of the USA also came via Spanish. Some are to do with the landscape: *canyon*, *chapparal* ('brushwood'), *mesa* ('table-land'), *sierra* (for jagged hills or mountains, and related to English 'serrated'; ultimately from Latin, *serra*: 'saw'). Some expressions carry the tang of the Wild West: *ranch*; *corral*; *desperado*; *sombrero*; *vigilante*; *bonanza* ('fair weather', and so 'prosperity', deriving ultimately from Latin, *bonus*: 'good'). Others are connected with animals or animal-handling: mustang (Spanish: *mestengo*); coyote; bronco ('rough/sturdy');* stampede

---

* Readers *d'un certain âge* will recall the shiny-sided lavatory paper which was marketed as Bronco. This was a British patent, and seems to be have been one of a clutch of toilet-tissue names connoting strength and toughness, including

(Spanish: *estampida*); lasso; lariat; rodeo. The ten-gallon hat, that essential perquisite of the swaggering cowboy or *vaquero*, has nothing to do with how much liquid the hat could hold, but is most likely a mishearing/mistranslation of the Spanish *galón* (braid) and so refers to the number of ornamental bands on the hat, which must still have been pretty big. Two other terms with Wild West associations are from other languages and have deeper roots: 'sheriff', ultimately from Old English (in translated form: *shire* + *reeve*), and 'posse', a shortened form of a Latinate phrase, *posse comitatus*, and used to describe the group of men legally required to answer a sheriff's summons to pursue escaping felons – not in the United States but in the England of the Middle Ages.

Samson and Bulldog. The Bronco line was discontinued in 1989. *Cloacapapyrology* is the proposed term (not yet in dictionaries) for the study of lavatory paper, in all its varieties. There is an interesting article on the subject on the Ephemera Society's website under the heading 'Sic transit gloria cloacarum'.

AUGUSTAN

≈ (1706) ≈

TWO MEMBERS OF THE most famous dynasty of Roman emperors – the Julio-Claudian line – left their linguistic mark on the English language. Augustus Caesar (63 BC–AD 14), the nephew and then adopted son to Julius, gives us 'Augustan' to describe his long and largely peaceful rule. Because it was an era in which literature flourished, the adjective was first used in 1706 to characterize Roman poetry, but later applied to the classical, decorous era of English writing, particularly poetry, in the eighteenth century. This most successful of emperors is also remembered for thirty-one days every year since August, once called *Sextilis* (i.e. the sixth month) in Rome, was renamed in 8 BC in tribute to him. Surprisingly, the charismatic and ruthless Julius Caesar (100–44 BC) provides no expression at all to do with warfare, politics or cunning, but only 'Caesarean' (section), first cited as far back as 1615 and now so familiar that it's just a C-section, so called because that's the way JC came into the world. Julius, however, imposed the calendrical system which bore his name (the Julian calendar) until it was replaced by the Gregorian calendar, not introduced into England until 1750 to align the country with western Europe. The rest of the Julio-Claudian dynasty are a ragged bunch, linguistically and otherwise: Shakespeare's contemporary John Florio refers to 'Neronian cruelties' (1598) while Horace Walpole, the creator of the term 'serendipity' (see page 203), coined 'Caligulism' in 1745 to describe someone's mad or extravagant action. The emperors referred to, Nero and Caligula, were bywords for cruelty, sexual violence and psychosis.

KETCHUP

≈ (1711) ≈

D IRECT BORROWINGS FROM CHINESE are rare in English, and only a small number of words could be described as well established. One such is **ketchup**, first noted in this anglicized spelling in 1711, and coming from the Amoy dialect, spoken in southeast China, although an alternative linguistic source (pun intended) in Malayan has also been posited. **Ketchup** used to be made from a mushroom base but tomatoes have long provided the most familiar ingredient and colour of the sauce. It has been a British staple for some time; both Byron and Dickens mention it. In the US it is often referred to as *catsup* but generally marketed as **ketchup**. Another food accompaniment, soy sauce, may be associated principally with Japan, but the word derives from two Chinese terms combining 'beans' (or a similar condiment) and 'oil'. A handful of food terms are unequivocally Chinese, such as *chop suey*, *chow mein* (literally, fried flour) and *dim sum*. Disconcertingly, there may be a link between *chow*, the Chinese-derived slang for food, and the canine breed known as chow, which has in the past been described as 'the edible dog of China'.

Other loans from China include *kowtow* which, drawing the two words for 'knock' and 'head' together, describes the custom of touching the forehead to the floor, a mark of respect or obeisance which unsettled some early European visitors to the Chinese court. The expression is familiar enough in English to signify behaviour which is excessively deferential but, with few people knowing the origin of the word and so unable to visualize the act, it doesn't convey much indignation. *Gung ho* is from two Chinese words meaning 'work together', and was adopted by the US Marine Corps as their motto during the Second World War. The word no longer suggests co-operation but has the sense of 'enthusiastic', even 'over-keen'. One of the minor linguistic distinctions between American and British English is that whereas in the former *gung ho* generally seems to indicate approval ('Her voter base does not seem as gung-ho energetic as Sanders's base.' *New York Times*), in the latter it often comes with a distinct note of scepticism ('We should feel proud of a Parliament that seeks to be cautious in matters of war and peace, rather than gung-ho.' *New Statesman*).

Another two-word combination is *feng-shui*, first appearing in English as *fong-choui* in 1797. Literally 'wind-water' the term describes the network of intangible spirit influences, good and bad, which operate in a place, and knowledge of which is necessary to find the most propitious site for a house, grave, etc. Whatever its near-mystical origins, the word seems to apply in the West mostly at the level of home-improvement. *Yin* and *yang* aren't treated with much respect in the English language, either. These terms, almost always appearing together as 'yin and yang', represent opposites that are at one and the same time opposed, complementary and inter-dependent. In Chinese philosophy, they stand for those cosmic forces whose inseparable duality is required to bring the world into being. *Yin* is the active female principle, sometimes identified with the moon, while *yang* is the male, sometimes signifying the sun. In general use, 'ying and yang' doesn't convey much more than 'good and bad', 'black and white'. There is a sometimes a hint of the underlying male / female duality, though it is not detectable in this quote from the *Guardian* about Manchester City: 'Touré is sensitive to scrutiny and would probably not appreciate being made an example of here, but it happens to be his lot that no one better epitomizes his team's yin and yang.'

MUMBO-JUMBO

≈ (1738) ≈

THE **MUMBO-JUMBO** WAS A supposed god worshipped by some West African peoples, the word probably deriving from *maamajomboo*, a term in Mandinka (the principal language of the Gambia), for a mask or a masked dancer who participated in cult ceremonies. But, in keeping with the more usual English sense of the word, **mumbo-jumbo** seems to have been little more than a con, and specifically a coercive trick practised on women by their husbands. The Scottish explorer Mungo Park detailed his findings in his *Travels in the Interior Districts of Africa* (1799), terming it 'a strange bugbear,*

---

* The word 'bugbear' for an imaginary terror has been around since the sixteenth century. The 'bear' bit is presumably because the imagined terror took an ursine shape, maybe in tales intended to frighten children, but the etymology of 'bug' is

common to all the Mandingo towns, and much employed by the Pagan natives in keeping their women in subjection.' According to Park, when the quarrels between a man's wives [sic] grew unmanageable, the enforcer was called in:

> This strange minister of justice (who is supposed to be either the husband himself, or some person instructed by him), disguised in the dress that has been mentioned, and armed with the rod of public authority, announces his coming (whenever his services are required) by loud and dismal screams in the woods near the town. […] The ceremony commences with songs and dances, which continue till midnight, about which time Mumbo fixes on the offender. This unfortunate victim being thereupon immediately seized, is stripped naked, tied to a post, and severely scourged with Mumbo's rod, amidst the shouts and derision of the whole assembly; and it is remarkable, that the rest of the women are the loudest in their exclamations on this occasion against their unhappy sister. Daylight puts an end to this indecent and unmanly revel.

---

less certain. In Middle English *bugge* meant 'an object of terror, probably unreal' and this may derive from Welsh. (One of the words for 'ghost' in modern Welsh is *bwgan*.) The various forms of *bug* could be related to *bogy/bogey* – as in 'the bogey man' – even though *bogy* is not recorded before the middle of the nineteenth century. The insect definition of *bug* came later than the 'hobgoblin' one.

The application of **mumbo-jumbo** (now generally in lower case) to nonsensical speech or as a synonym for 'nonsense' appears in the nineteenth century, and the term is still quite regularly found. It characterizes things that are meant to impress but have no real substance to them. **Mumbo-jumbo** joins a list of other terms in which two words are put together in a kind of double act, the second echoing the first usually with a small variation, in a linguistic process whose technical name is reduplication. When these doubles are applied to speech or action they almost always denote suspicion or even contempt: arty-farty, jibber jabber, chitter chatter, jaw jaw, hocus pocus, flim-flam, hanky panky. Another synonym for nonsense, 'claptrap', looks and sounds like a reduplication but in its original eighteenth-century usage described a stage trick or device intended to provoke applause or 'trap the clap', and hence came to signify something 'showy' and therefore 'worthless'.

GAUCHE

∽ (1751) ∾

HISTORY, LANGUAGE AND CUSTOM favour not just the right-handed but the right side altogether. The clumsy dancer or mover has two left feet, never two right ones. In retelling the story of creation in *Paradise Lost*, John Milton has God fashioning Eve – the 'weaker sex' – from a rib taken out of Adam's left side, even though no particular side is specified in Genesis. In 2016 a little flurry of fuss and interest – predictably dubbed 'sofa-gate' – followed the observation that when there are two presenters, one male, one female, on British TV news programmes and especially on the morning sofa-based shows, the man is almost invariably seated to the right of the woman. Although this is the left side from the viewers' point of view, research suggest that those same viewers identify with the right-hand side from the presenters' point of view, as if they themselves were sitting on that sofa, and that they associate 'rightness' with seniority and authority.

The implication is that whatever lies on the right is stronger, more auspicious, more dextrous (from Latin *dexter*: 'on the right[-hand] side') than what is on the left. This hasn't always been the case, or at least not everywhere. In fact, the Romans regarded the left side as the more favourable one, partly because it was nearer to the heart. They turned southwards when taking auspices (from *avis* + *specere*: 'bird' + 'to watch'), so that their left was angled to the east or fortunate quarter, and they regarded birds flying from left to right as more propitious than the ones flying right to left. But, in general, the few terms deriving from Latin and connected with the right or right-handedness suggest grace and skill: 'dextrous' has already been mentioned and someone who is physically adept with both hands is said to be 'ambidextrous', i.e. as if in possession of two right hands. There is also 'adroit', from French *à droit*, with a meaning that is less to do with 'going right' than with 'being in the right', and so 'deft', 'skilful'. The opposite of adroit is maladroit, or clumsy.

On the other hand, so to speak, there are plenty of terms associated with the left side and left-handedness that connote clumsiness or ill fortune, not just in English but other European languages. In Italian *manco*, one of the words for 'left', is related to *mancare* (to be wanting, insufficient). In French, **gauche** is the standard word for 'left'* but also means 'clumsy', 'awkward', as it does in English, and was first noted in this sense when used by Lord Chesterfield in one of his letters to his son, advising on manners and behaviour. (Chesterfield was also the patron who Dr Johnson hoped to get for his great *Dictionary*, and whose interest came too late and prompted a famously cold and angry letter from the lexicographer.) *Gaucherie*, found occasionally in English, denotes a general awkwardness in either language.

While the left side may have been an auspicious one for the Romans, their word for it – *sinister* – was already by the early fifteenth century being used in English in dubious, pejorative contexts; a little later it takes on the sense of 'ominous', 'inauspicious', so reversing the Roman belief about the lucky side. There are several English dialect terms for left-handedness including 'keg-handed', 'corrie-fisted' and 'cack-handed'. These convey clumsiness, and the last is probably related to the excremental sense of 'cack',† in that

---

* What is gauche can also be chic, at least in France. The *Rive Gauche* (Left Bank of the Seine) in Paris was the district linked to artists, philosophers and bohemians, the inter-war world of Picasso, Sartre and Hemingway. Now it's the name of an up-market scent. One other slightly positive 'left' reference comes in the US baseball term 'left field'. Metaphorically speaking, 'left field' ideas, etc. may be unusual or creative.

† Also at the root of the innocuous-sounding exclamation 'Poppycock!' which comes from the not-so-clean Dutch *pappekak* (soft dung).

the left hand is in some cultures, including Islam, the one reserved for cleaning oneself after defecation. Altogether, it can be said that left-handers have not had an easy linguistic time of it.

SERENDIPITY

≈ (1754) ≈

T HIS IS A PECULIAR word for two reasons. One is
the oddity of its conception and the other is that,
in effect, it disappeared for around two hundred
years before turning into a must-have item in the linguistic handbag. Richard Boyle, the author of *Knox's Words*
(2004),* observes that by 1958 **serendipity** had been used
in print only 135 times, but that between then and 2000 it
featured in the title of 57 books. According to the US Boat
Owners Association, it is the tenth most popular name
for a pleasure craft. A glance at any newspaper website

---

* The full title is: *Knox's Words: A Study of the Words of Sri Lankan Origin or Asso-*
ciation First Used in English Literature by Robert Knox and Recorded in the Oxford
English Dictionary. Robert Knox (1641–1720) was the first person to write a book
in English about Ceylon, now Sri Lanka.

will show hundreds of usages both of **serendipity** and its equally popular adjectival form 'serendipitous'. This, from the *Spectator*, is representative and more or less illustrates its meaning: 'It's been a week of serendipitous moments on radio, surprising, memorable, moving [...] the magic of hearing something or someone you didn't at all expect and would never have chosen to listen to.'

First, the word's conception. It was the coinage of Horace Walpole, the son of the first British prime minister Robert Walpole. More to the point, Walpole was the creator of the Gothic ice-cream which is Strawberry Hill House in Twickenham and the author of *The Castle of Otranto* (1764), a quirky supernatural story generally reckoned to be the earliest novel in the Gothic genre (castle, caves, woods, knights, maidens). Ten years before *Otranto*, in a letter to a friend, Walpole, who was also a historian and collector, described how he'd made a happy but unexpected discovery to do with heraldry and coats-of-arms. It was a discovery, he explained, 'almost of that kind which I call Serendipity.' Walpole enlarged on what he meant:

'I once read a silly fairy tale, called The Three Princes of Serendip [the original name for Ceylon, or Sri Lanka]: as their Highnesses travelled, they were always making discoveries, by accidents and sagacity, of things which they were not in quest of: for instance, one of them discovered that a mule blind of the right eye had travelled the same road lately, because the grass was eaten only on the left side, where it was worse than on the right – now do you understand Serendipity?'

It has been claimed that Walpole's own example is not a particularly good case of **serendipity**, since it involves a Holmes-style piece of deduction rather than the discovery of something (useful, valuable) when you are actually in quest of something else. Nevertheless, as the inventor of the word, Walpole must have some claim to know what he meant. Its function in scientific research has often been noted, as in this 1955 quotation from *Scientific American*: 'discovery often depends on chance, or rather on what has been called "serendipity" – the chance observation falling on a receptive eye'. Alexander's Fleming's discovery of penicillin is often cited as a prime instance of **serendipity** since he came across the bacteria-killing mould by accident. The key element, though, was Fleming's scientific training and his open-mindedness and curiosity about what he observed. **Serendipity** doesn't just describe a lucky find, but one which the finder has the intelligence to recognize as such.

The reason the word and its offshoot serendipitous, first used as late as 1958, have become so popular in the last half-century is a little harder to explain. Part of it is probably to do with the increasing recognition of the role that accident and chance play in scientific discovery. Part of it is surely connected to the sound of the word, the enticing, gentle, even serene opening syllable and the lip-smacking 'dip' in the middle. With its suggestion of good fortune, if not magic, it has a natural appeal to ad-men, brand managers and PR persons, even if in the process the original Walpolian sense has been eroded to mean not much more than a 'nice stroke of luck'. And finally, there is just the fact that any particular word may have its own inexplicable moment; and **serendipity** has certainly been having quite a long one.

KAYAK

≈ (1757) ≈

F
EWER THAN FORTY TERMS have found their way
into English from the Eskimo or In(n)uit tongues,
spoken by the original inhabitants of Greenland,
Canada and Alaska, and of these only a small handful are
in anything like regular use. The word Eskimo itself has
been superseded by Innuit or Inuit, which means no more
than 'people' in the Inuit language.

A couple of Inuit-derived expressions in English came
into the language several hundred years ago, brought back
by explorers and traders. 'Igloo' is one, **kayak** another. The
kayak is a one-person boat, and that person is generally
male to judge by the distinction drawn between it and the
larger *umiak*, which according to one nineteenth-century
observer in Greenland was a boat 'worked exclusively by

the women'. By contrast, two items of arctic clothing – 'anorak' and 'parka' – have entered popular consciousness quite recently. The anorak seems to hail from Greenland where, far from being a functional and rather anonymous garment, it can form part of the national dress or even a *trousseau*. In 1936 a bride was described as wearing scarlet boots, sealskin trousers, and 'anoraq with magnificent bead collar'. More recent is the derogatory British English sense of anorak, meaning either a studious person or, more usually, a solitary obsessive, the equivalent to the US nerd or geek. Parka ('skin coat'), on the other hand, comes from thousands of miles away, and originates with the Nenets people of northern Siberia.

There is no Inuit-derived word for 'snow' in English but that hasn't stopped the popular belief growing up that speakers of the language have dozens, even hundreds, of such terms, on the shaky logic that they spend so much of their time with the stuff. It is not true. Anyone wanting an energetic debunking of a language myth should look up online 'The Great Eskimo Vocabulary Hoax' by Geoffrey Pullum or, also by Pullum, the entry in *Language Log* (15 January 2013) under the heading 'Bad Science Reporting Again: The Eskimos are back' or a satirical list by Phil James entitled 'The Eskimos' Hundred Words for Snow' and including such gems as *wa-ter* (melted snow) or *fritla* (fried snow).

SANDWICH

∽ (1762) ∾

I N 1765 A FRENCH historian and travel writer, Pierre-
Jean Grosley, spent some time in London, and for the
benefit of his countrymen he wrote an account of his
time there. The book went down well with the English too
when it was translated by Thomas Nugent a few years later.
One of Grosley's observations was about the popularity of
a newish form of fast food. In Nugent's version, it reads:

> A minister of state passed four and twenty hours at a public gam-
> ing-table, so absorpt in play that, during the whole time, he had
> no subsistence but a bit of beef, between two slices of toasted
> bread, which he eat without ever quitting the game. This new
> dish grew highly in vogue, during my residence in London: it
> was called by the name of the minister who invented it.

The minister of state was John Montagu, who held several government posts including First Lord of the Admiralty. Montagu may not have had a great name as a politician, but the inherited title which he held – the Earl of Sandwich – bequeathed two names to the world: South Sandwich Islands in the South Atlantic (the name given by Captain Cook as a nod to his Admiralty master), and the **sandwich** proper. Even if what Sandwich ate at the gaming table sounds more like a toasted **sandwich**, he is popularly credited with having brought into English a word which for most people now evokes a slice of tarted-up meat or cheese between two bits of untoasted bread, the whole thing snuggled into a cellophane-and-cardboard holster. There's an earlier reference than Grosley's in the *OED*, which quotes a 1762 passage from Edward Gibbon's journals in which he observes some of the 'first men in the kingdom' at the Cocoa Tree Club (the name testifies to the fashionable craze for chocolate houses in eighteenth-century London) dining on 'a bit of cold meat, or a Sandwich'. John Montague did not invent the idea of the **sandwich**, but his devotion to it or perhaps just his reluctance to leave the gaming table, ensured the word passed into history.

Sandwich is an eponymous term but it's distinct from some other eponymous examples in this book (like **Stalinist** or **Bowdlerize**, see pages 307 and 250) in that it is a noun, rather than an adjective or verb, and is in effect a proper name applied directly to an object, invention or process. Other food-related examples include Beef Wellington, probably named in honour of the victor of Waterloo and following a vogue for attaching his name to items such as boots, to which a Beef Wellington bears a vague sort of resemblance in shape. The tortilla chip or nacho is supposed to derive from the diminutive version of Ignacio Anaya's first name. A Mexican chef during the 1940s, Ignacio invented the snack when a group of women down from Texas asked for something to accompany their cocktails. Also from Mexico and from around the same period emerged the Caesar salad, the creation of Caesar Cardini, Italian-born but running a restaurant in Tijuana. The Australian soprano Nellie Melba – her stage-name taken from her birthplace of Melbourne – is commemorated in two items that might **sandwich** a meal: melba toast, a good accompaniment to pâté, and peach Melba, equally good to finish with.

Other direct-name eponyms include: biro, braille, hoover, tupperware (from Earl Tupper, not an English milord but an inventor from New England); car marques such as Ford, Rolls-Royce, Porsche, Lamborghini and Chrysler; and diseases or conditions named after those involved in their discovery (Alzheimer's, Parkinson's) or those afflicted by them (Lou Gehrig's disease). Then there is a range of plants named after distinguished botanists: dahlia, buddleia, fuchsia (Dahl, Buddle and Fuchs). Scientific units of measurement frequently commemorate their discoverers, among them Volt, Ohm and Fahrenheit. Oil men might be surprised to discover that their derricks are named after a noted executioner at London's Tyburn, close to what is now Marble Arch. From an Elizabethan hangman surnamed Derrick to the scaffold he operated on is a short step.

It's also common to find a proper name, usually in its complete form, used to describe an action, remark, etc. which is seen as characteristic of some exemplar, as in 'He did a Lord Lucan' or 'He may be dishonest but there's a bit of the Robin Hood about him' or 'She gave him her Margaret Thatcher stare.'

XXXXXXX

⁓ (1763) ⁓

E VEN A SINGLE LETTER in the alphabet may take on a symbolic value, and no letter is more evocative, ambiguous and versatile than the x. When capitalized, Mr or Ms X may be the tantalisingly unnamed party to some dispute or court case, while X marks the spot on a map but gives no clue at all to what lies beneath. Your X on the ballot paper is an assertion of a democratic right, but the X on a different piece of paper can also be the mark of what's wrong (the counterpart of the tick). For years after its introduction in 1950, the X-rating for films – the precursor to the current '18' age-restriction in the United Kingdom – was a combination of warning and come-on. Often the X was proclaimed in bigger, bolder type than the title or the stars and even multiplied

(XX, XXX!) to show that this wasn't just adult material but ADULT.

And then there are the multiples of x for kisses. Usually lower case and subject to the same inflationary effect as the taboo X, their origin is also mysterious. One suggestion is that the crossed lines of the letter represents crossed lips, but whatever the source x has represented a way of signing-off since at least 1763, when the naturalist Gilbert White used a string of them to finish a letter. However, the context in which White's x-string occurs also includes a reference to 'many a Pater noster and Ave Maria' (White was a parson), so it is possible that the writer was invoking blessings rather than kisses. Yet another symbolic value of the x-shape is that in Greek the letter X is represented in English as 'Chi', the first letter for Christ.

LACKADAISICAL

≈ (1768) ≈

ACKADAISICAL MEANS 'LANGUISHING', 'LACKING in energy or effort'. It is first used by the clergyman-novelist Laurence Sterne in *Sentimental Journey* in a spelling which seems to mimic the tiredness of the writer: 'lack-a-day-sical'. The adjective comes from 'lack-adaisy', which comes from 'lack-a-day' which comes from the phrase 'alack the day'* or, in an earlier version, 'alas the day', initially used to register regret or sadness at events on

---

* The process by which 'alack the day' loses its first letter and becomes 'lackaday' is known as *aphesis* (from Greek and literally a 'letting go'). A number of familiar English words have been formed by *aphesis*, which tends to occur when the opening vowel is unstressed and can be dispensed with. They include squire (from esquire), cute (acute), mend (amend), fence (defence). Colloquial shortenings, like 'cause (or cos) for because, ' scuse, 'spose and 's'alright are examples of the same process. And 'example' has produced its own aphetic form in 'sample', both words signifying something taken out of a larger group.

a particular day, and later as a more generalized expression of concern. In turn, 'alas' derives from a combination of two elements of Old French: *a/ah*, an interjection signifying pity, etc. and *las* ('unhappy, weary'). *Las* goes back to the Latin *lassus* or 'tired', as in 'lassitude', identical in both modern French and English.

'Alas' is an example of an interjection (see also **hum**, page 128), a curious linguistic category that stands at a slight angle to regular parts of speech. In a sense, interjections – ah!, boo!, d'oh, hey!, ooh, phew, uh-oh, and dozens of others – are more primal than the words classified under headings like noun or pronoun or adverb. They have something in common with animal sounds, and although comparatively few in number they make up a disproportionate part of our speech. Interjections tend to be ironed out in writing, except in fictional dialogue, and even there their use is restricted. But a glance at any real conversation which has been recorded and transposed, say for legal purposes, shows how crammed everyday speech is with hesitations, exclamations, expressions of doubt and disbelief, fillers like 'like', 'well' and 'ok', as well as non-verbal utterances in the form of sighs, gasps, gulps, tuts and groans.

Interjections share these features: they are much more frequently found in speech than writing; they are uttered involuntarily or at least without much thought; they generally lack in etymological origins. They often work as space-fillers in speech, occupying the time while we formulate a more coherent response. Despite these seeming limitations, they are highly expressive and versatile words. Indeed, a single one may reveal more than a page of prose or a carefully prepared public utterance.

Take 'Ah'. Depending on the context and tone of voice in which it's said, Ah can signal surprise, realization, pleasure, pity, dejection, objection ('ah but…'). Adding an exclamation mark, Ah!, restricts the emotional range slightly, to delight or discovery, but it intensifies the response. Putting in an extra a- before the -h turns it into a cry of pain – Aah (or Aaaah for emphasis, or a fall off a cliff). Putting an additional -a after the -h produces a Sherlock Holmes-style moment of insight – Aha! Many other interjections are just as adaptable as ah, with oh perhaps the most versatile of all.

Their usefulness extends a little further because they also add to the stock of English words when they are incorporated and formalized into 'proper' parts of speech. **Lackadaisical** is one such example. Another is that historic feature of the landscape of a country estate, the ha-ha, the word first recorded in 1724. This trench-like boundary, usually between the formal part of a garden or park and the less-cultivated land beyond, consists of a stone-walled drop of several feet on the garden side and a gentler grass slope on the opposite one. The function of the ha-ha is to allow an uninterrupted view from inside the grand house – no visible fences, walls or barriers, nothing but flowing countryside. The word comes from French and its first version in eighteenth-century England is the reversed 'Ah, Ah'. Whichever way round it goes, however, the ha-ha is so named for the gasp of surprise or laughter in the person discovering it. It might be supposed that possession of a ha-ha would give one a 'la-di-da' attitude, one that is a bit nose-in-the-air and superior, and an expression from the late Victorian period. But la-di-da – deriving onomatopoeically from the speech-style of someone acting posh – signifies what is genteel rather than classy. 'Haw haw' has similarly been taken as a marker of upper-class speech, hence the mocking nickname of Lord Haw-Haw applied to the plummy-voiced William Joyce, who broadcast fascist propaganda from Germany to Britain during the Second World War.

Another interjection that has become regularized in speech as a noun is 'hurrah/hooray' in phrases such as 'the last hurrah' (originally the title of a 1956 US novel and applied to a politician's final campaign, now used about any last appearance), and 'Hooray Henry' for a braying upper-class nit; though generally assumed to be British, it in fact emanated from America and a 1936 story by Damon Runyon. A dab of 'ooh-la-la' (French: *oh là là*) has for years evoked a whole world of French 'naughtiness'; the headline for a *Guardian* article about French farce sums it up:

'Ooh-la-la, there go my trousers.' Then there's 'blah', to deride meaningless talk, and often appearing in triplicate: blah blah blah. This works like the dismissive US yadda yadda yadda ('yackety-yak'). 'Yum', expressing pleasure, has been around since Victorian times, often duplicated to 'yum-yum' for something good to eat but also standing for sex. The 'yummy mummy' was first noted in a Canadian newspaper in 1993.

Two comparative newcomers to the stock of interjections are worth mentioning: 'like', because it is ubiquitous, and 'meh', because it has become the nearest thing to an interjection *du jour*. If it's hard to pinpoint the moment when like became indispensable as a filler, an early use of the word in Robert Louis Stevenson's novel *Kidnapped* comes as a surprise: '"What's like wrong with him?" said she at last.' This was in 1886. There are intermittent instances of the word being used in this way in the next century – that is, meaninglessly – but it is not until the 1980s that like becomes not so much an occasional conversational filler but the very mortar that holds teen-speak together. 'I was, like, you want to go or not?' 'He was like, yeah, whatever.' Its frequency has been linked with the rise of 'upspeech' or 'uptalk', the way in which the voice of the speaker, usually a young speaker, will rise in a questioning way at the end of declarative sentence, so that a statement such as 'I went to the Isle of Wight(?)' seems to ask for the listener's agreement that such a visit was acceptable or even perhaps a plea to confirm that the Isle of Wight exists. The very widespread use of like and the uptalking habit have been attributed not just to fashion and imitation but to uncertainty, whether verbal or social, on the part of a younger generation.

Meh, denoting 'So what?', was popularized by *The Simpsons*, and may derive from Yiddish. Its simplicity as an interjection and its expressiveness as an adjective ('It's a bit meh') to indicate mediocrity have given these three letters widespread currency, though it is more popular in the US than the UK, where meh may still appear in quote marks or as an example of 'internet parlance'. No such scruples in America, where Donald Trump, in the early stages of his campaign for the White House in January 2016, said of a US–Iran deal: 'So essentially they get 150 billion plus seven [released prisoners], and we get four. Meh, doesn't sound too good. Doesn't sound too good.'

KANGAROO

≈ (c.1770) ≈

ONE OF THE CREW members on Captain Cook's boat had a question when the expedition arrived at the east coast of Australia in 1770. Pointing to one of the peculiar beasts that abounded – and bounded – in the area, the sailor asked an aborigine for its name. 'Kangaroo,' was the reply, or 'I can't understand you.' Hence the name of Australia's most famous marsupial is based on a mistranslation. The story sounds too good to be true, and so it is. An anthropological study in the early 1970s of an aboriginal community living near Cook's original landing place established that the name in their language for the beast was *gangurru*. It seems that this applied to a particular type of large grey **kangaroo**, but it's easy to see how the name was altered slightly and then applied to all types of **kangaroo.** This was only one of several indigenous names for the beast, and indeed other aboriginal communities didn't recognize the word, some of them assuming they were being taught the *English* name for the animal when they first heard it. The aborigines did not speak a single language but several, and as with the early European settlers of America there was a constant tendency to simplify and underestimate indigenous culture.

The contribution of the native Australian languages to English is small and largely restricted to those animals and plants that weren't familiar to the first European arrivals, like the koala and wallaby. These two, together with **kangaroo**, dingo and boomerang, appear among the ten most common aboriginal terms. Of these, only the boomerang and more especially the kangaroo have acquired figurative legs, with the creature popping up in American metaphors from the mid-nineteenth century onwards in phrases such as 'kangaroo court' – for which no satisfactory derivation has ever been found – or 'kangaroo ticket', used to describe the duo campaigning for the White House when the man standing for vice-president was seen as a better prospect than the one aspiring to be president. (The virtue of such a campaign was said to reside, like the animal's strength, in its hind legs.) The metaphorical arrival of the **kangaroo** in America coincided with the arrival of many Australians in California during the gold rush.

TABU

∽ (1777) ∾

I T WASN'T ONLY IN **Australia** that Captain Cook's voyagers encountered words that would eventually filter into English (see **kangaroo**). In the years between 1768 and 1776, James Cook made three exploratory voyages to the southern hemisphere, and Tahiti was one of his landfalls. On his arrival at the island he observed how the indigenous islanders decorated their bodies by covering them with indelible markings. The original Polynesian word is *tatau,* and in the eighteenth century it entered English as *tatt(a)ow* before settling into its current form of 'tattoo'.*

---

* The military sense of 'tattoo', referring to the evening drum-beat or bugle call summoning soldiers back to camp or barracks, has nothing to do with body painting. Instead it comes from a Dutch phrase meaning 'turn off the tap' and so 'stop' or 'shut up'.

A more significant cultural discovery made by Cook was the extensive **tabu** system that rendered certain things inviolable or forbidden. A 'taboo', the more usual and later spelling, might prevent women from entering a particular place or it could restrict the topics available for discussion. The awareness in all societies of practices which are prohibited less by law than by social custom, as well as the existence of language which is offensive and so taboo, means that this is a term useful not only to linguists, anthropologists and sociologists but one that has widespread currency. The German title of Sigmund Freud's *Totem und Tabu* (1913) scarcely needs translating and indicates how readily these two 'anthropological' terms from opposite sides of the world were adopted by different Western languages. But the word has also been frequently used for film, television and book titles. This teasing use of taboo may not be very subtle but it points to the fact that what is forbidden is also enticing.

A restricted number of terms have crossed into the English language from the countries that dot or border the vast area of the world that is the Pacific Ocean. Unlike tattoo and taboo, most are fairly obscure and relate to the flora and fauna of the region. One of the more curious words is 'ukelele', the miniature four-stringed guitar out of Hawaii which in turn developed from the 'machete' – not the knife but an instrument originally imported from

Portugal. The music-hall star George Formby played with the ukelele in both senses, strumming it on stage and punning suggestively on the name of the thing. (They may be mild by current standards but worth a look are the full lyrics of his famous 'With My Little Ukelele in My Hand', a companion piece to his 'With My Little Stick of Blackpool Rock'.) The ukelele is not found in English before 1896, and its origin appears to lie in a combination of two Hawaiian words for 'flea' and 'jumping'. It's open to question whether this describes the rapid movement of fingers over the strings or whether, as one quotation suggests, it derives from the small stature and jerky antics of a particular player. Another imported musical term is *gamelan*, from Java, applying to a percussion ensemble. The gentle gonglike tones of the *gamelan* style have been used by Western composers from Debussy to Benjamin Britten.

Another possible linguistic import from the Pacific region is curious because the product has always been associated with Jamaica and the Caribbean. The *Oxford English Dictionary* suggests tentatively that 'rum'* may have a Malay origin in a term for rice spirit (*beram*), and takes a sideways

---

* The drinkable rum is not connected with 'rum' in the sense of 'odd', 'peculiar' ('a rum do', 'a rum cove'). This adjectival rum possibly derives from an earlier sense of the word to mean 'high quality', 'excellent', and if so it is an interesting example of a word which can flip meaning like a tossed coin, as with 'wicked' in current use.

look at the now-obsolete terms *rumbullion* and *rumbustion*, both signifying the drink. But the link between these and other rum-related terms is complicated and, on the face of it, it seems more likely that the word rum, like the product, had its origins in the Western rather than the Eastern hemisphere. Some other expressions which are indisputably Malay include 'gong', an onomatopoeic term; 'caddy', the box for holding tea and probably a corruption of *catty/kati*, a unit of weight amounting to about two-thirds of a kilo; 'paddy', as in field (*padi*: 'rice'); 'orangutan' ('person of the forest'); animals like the 'gecko' lizard, the 'pangolin' or anteater, and that strange sea-going mammal, the 'dugong'; and indigenous birds such as the 'cassowary', 'lory' and 'cockatoo'.

One of the most frequently found Malayan borrowings is *amok*, from *amoq*, and common in the English phrase 'running amok', in use since the seventeenth century to describe someone who is out of control, and possibly violent. Early references suggest amok might have referred to do-or-die fighters in battle, but others describe individuals who go into a frenzy as a result of taking 'a deleterious drug' (opium?) or simply ascribe the condition of being amok to Malayan culture, a kind of local insanity. Rather like the similar expression 'going berserk' – deriving from reckless Norse warriors who fought either in bear-skin (bear-sark) or bare-shirt (unarmoured) – 'running amok' has largely lost contact with its exotic, murderous origins.

A couple of slang terms come from Pacific languages. Malagasy, the national language of Madagascar, provides the 'drongo', properly the name of a fly-catching bird, but in Australian slang a characteristically expressive term for someone slow-witted. It may be, though, that the word doesn't come directly from the bird but was instead the name of an Australian racehorse that consistently came in last or next to last, and so achieved its own kind of fame. From Tagalog, one of the languages of the Philippines, comes the US semi-slang term *boondock* (a *bundok* is a hill or mountain), sometimes shortened in the phrase 'in the boonies'. With much the same meaning as 'in the sticks' or 'backwoods', it was picked up by American fighters in the Philippines during the Spanish–American War of 1898. The boondocks are not necessarily mountainous but they are always a long way from the city, sparsely populated, and as usual with such country references regarded as being somewhat backward.

PLACEBO

❧ (1785) ❧

PLACEBO IS A TERM now used in medicine to describe a sham drug or other form of treatment such as a sugar pill or a saline injection which, though having no real physiological or biological effect, may provide some psychological benefit because patients believe the treatment to be doing them good. It first surfaces in a medical context in 1785 as an entry in a medical dictionary, which would suggest that it was already established in such a sense, but the expression has a much older history. As the future tense form of *placere* ('to please'), **placebo** has the literal meaning in Latin of 'I shall be pleasing.' It's in this sense, as 'I shall be acceptable', that it figures in the Catholic Office of the Dead. During the Middle Ages and later on, the word denoted a flatterer.

In *The Merchant's Tale* (*c.*1395?), Chaucer introduces a wealthy old knight, symbolically named January, pondering marriage to a much younger woman, symbolically named May. One of his counsellors, Justinus, tells him that this is a bad idea. The other, called Placebo, lives up to his name by saying '*Dooth now in this matiere right as yow leeste* [please]/*For finally I holde it for the beste.*' Justinus is right to be dubious, as January goes blind and is then cuckolded when May joins her lover to have sex in a pear-tree (see also **jargon**, page 61).

The **placebo** effect in medicine is well attested, and seems to extend even to trusted brand names. A US study on the benefit of headache pills which involved students as guinea-pigs found that, of those given **placebo** pills which were either generic (ibuprofen) or branded (Nurofen), more reported feeling better after taking what they believed was the brand-name remedy. Another dubiously curative word from Latin is *nostrum*, deriving from *noster* ('our'), and applied to anything which is supposed to have healing properties but is probably no more than a short-term fix, if that. The source of the word seems to be a shortening of a phrase such as *nostrum remedium* or 'remedy of ours', the kind of thing that a quack seller of medicines might say, in Latin, to impress his customers. The word is often used in economic and political commentary and, like the comparable *panacea* ('cure-all': Greek) and **placebo**, it almost always sounds a sceptical note: 'We're just trotting out the same old nostrums: a little class warfare here and a nod to labor unions there and more money for X, Y and Z programs.' (*Politico*)

PANOPTICON

≈ (1790) ≈

VISITORS TO UNIVERSITY COLLEGE, London, can see a man in a glass case, a so-called 'auto-icon'. It is Jeremy Bentham (1748–1832). A visionary and progressive figure, Bentham wrote about the law, religion, prison reform and much else. He introduced the ethical/philosophical notion of utilitarianism, the belief that the greatest happiness of the greatest number should be the guiding principle of action. In his will he left specific instructions for the disposal of his body which, after preservation, was to be encased in a box and then from time to time brought into a room where his friends or disciples might meet to commemorate 'the founder of the greatest happiness system of morals and legislation'. The body on view at University College, which regards him as one of its founding fathers, consists of his preserved skeleton, dressed in his own clothes and topped by a wax head. Bentham had planned that the head on display should be his own, but the results of trying to preserve it using a process of desiccation practised by the Maoris were, in the words of the University College website, 'decidedly unattractive'. However, Bentham's wishes were not completely thwarted because the actual head, complete with glass eyes, was for many years displayed between Bentham's legs on the floor of the display cabinet before graduating to its own purpose-built box on top of the cabinet. (Views on the ethics of displaying human remains have changed and the head is now locked away in a safe in the Institute of Archaeology, where permission to inspect it will be granted only in 'exceptional circumstances'.)

There is an aptness to the fact that Bentham's body, or part of it, is on display to the public, and that he wanted this to be so. His most famous social/philosophical creation apart from utilitarianism was the **panopticon**, a design for a prison which originated with Jeremy's brother, Samuel, who created such a building in St Petersburg (though it was a school rather than a prison). The word, coming from a combination of two Greek words and meaning 'all-seeing', was already in English use but only to refer to a peep-show device that offered views of townscapes, etc. for public entertainment. Bentham's purpose, though, was a very serious one. In his **panopticon** or 'Inspection House', the cells would be arranged around a central well from which the occupants could be viewed at all times. The designs look something like the cross-section of an orange. The 'inspector' in the centre would even be able to speak to the prisoners via speaking tubes, though they wouldn't be able to see him and, crucially, could never know whether they were being watched or not. Not only would this be an economical scheme, Bentham argued, but it would improve the inmates' health and morals and their industriousness. A patch of land was bought next to the Thames on Millbank, where Tate Britain now stands, but the penitentiary eventually constructed there was not a **panopticon**. Some prisons were built to Bentham's pattern. To get an idea of what one looks like – a rather grim, unnerving look – search for online images of Stateville Penitentiary in Joliet, Illinois.

◈

TOTEM

≈ (1791) ≈

AMONG THE INDIGENOUS AMERICANS, a **totem** was the badge or mark of a tribe or clan, most usually in the representation of animals like the eagle, otter, bear, buffalo, and so on. The totemic animal, having an affinity with the tribe and passed down through the generations, may be looked on as a kind of guardian angel. The word first appears in English in 1791, though there is a reference nearly 200 years earlier to an '*aoutem*'.

The English-speaking settlers in northeast America simplified and adopted a number of words from the Indian*

---

* Not only is the term 'Indian' now seen as dated, disparaging and border-line racist, it is also a famous misnomer. Christopher Columbus, believing that he had reached the Indian Ocean when he arrived in the West Indies [sic], called the indigenous people Indians. Although the error was soon realized, the name stuck.

languages, most obviously those for animals which were unfamiliar to them such as the moose, skunk and raccoon, as well as the occasional food- or drink-related item like squash, pecan, hickory and potlatch (originally a winter festival but now applicable in the US to any gift-giving occasion/feast) and hooch (from the low-grade alcohol made by the Hoochinoo people of Alaska). Items at first unfamiliar in the shape of the tomahawk, toboggan, moccasin, tepee and wigwam (first cited in 1624) quickly established themselves in the settlers' language. These have survived over the centuries, along with terms that were always disparaging and which now border on the offensive such as squaw, papoose ('baby'), and fire-water (for any strong alcoholic drink and supposedly a translation of an Algonquin word).

Another term first recorded in English in 1624, like the wigwam, is what might have gone on inside one. *Powoh* or 'powwow', from an Algonquin language, originally had the meaning of 'sorcerer' or 'medicine man', before being applied to a ritual meeting, and hence to any kind of get-together or discussion between two or more parties. A more serious discussion is suggested by 'caucus', probably deriving from an indigenous word for 'talk to', 'give advice', but now used widely in the US to apply to a state or ethnic group – or sometimes just a bunch of insiders – which has a determining role in choosing a party's candidate for election. Lewis Carroll has fun with the word in *Alice's Adventures in Wonderland* (1865) where a caucus-race is run in a rough sort of circle, presided over by the Dodo. The contestants start where they like, stop when they please, and everyone gets a prize at the end. The point of it all eludes Alice. Yes, there are definite parallels with the American caucus process. Another term which might well have come from the pen of Lewis Carroll is *mugwump*. In fact, it's a Natick Indian word connoting 'great chief' and signified a political independent and specifically a Republican who in the 1884 election refused to support the Republican Party nominee for president on the grounds that he was financially corrupt. Arguably, caucuses and mugwumps aside, the most significant indigenous contribution to (US) English lies in place names. Many towns and cities, together with the great majority of the states, from Alabama to Wyoming, have names with native American origins. The exceptions, like New Jersey and New Hampshire, are obvious.

MURPHY

≈ (1811) ≈

MURPHY IS SLANG FOR potato and an almost obsolete term now. Since it's also a very common surname in Ireland, the word makes a derogatory link between the people of that country and the crop that was once a staple of their diet. If it's any comfort the origin of the Irish surname is more elevated than a potato clamp since it derives from a word meaning 'descendant of a sea-warrior'. **Murphy** joins a small clutch of expressions which, in a mildly abusive style, link a nation with one of its traditional foods. So 'kraut' for German, after *sauerkraut* (literally 'sour [pickled] cabbage), 'rosbif' and 'limey' for British (a shortened form of 'lime-juicer', so called on account of the limes given to British sailors to prevent scurvy), and 'macaroni' for Italian.

Murphy rears his head again in the US expression 'to play the murphy', describing a confidence trick whereby a man is enticed to a secluded spot with the promise of sex, only to be robbed; the slang lexicographer, Jonathon Green, raises the possibility that 'practitioners promised the victim a meeting with a lovely woman called Mrs Murphy'. But far the best-known modern incarnation of **Murphy** is in his eponymous law, which states that if anything can go wrong, it will. It's widely agreed that there must have been a Murphy to lend his name to the law in the first place, but which Murphy was it exactly? The generally accepted version dates from the late 1940s and has USAF Captain Edward Murphy in charge of tests on the gravitational effect of rapid deceleration on pilots. After his assistant wired gauges measuring the experiments the wrong way round, Murphy supposedly said something like, 'If there's a way of doing a job which ends in disaster then someone, sooner or later, is going to do it that way.' A different story suggests Murphy was not real but a character in US Navy educational cartoons, a careless, incompetent mechanic prone to mistakes such as installing a propellor backwards. In this version, Murphy's Law*

---

* It was the Australian John Bangsund who came up with the witty linguistic coinage of 'Muphry's Law' to describe how, if you set out as an editor to highlight someone else's written errors, you will inevitably make ones of your own. Copyeditors and others will recognise the rueful truth in the various clauses of

is more of a warning to be vigilant than a wry comment on human activity.

Muphry's Law, including this one: 'If an author thanks you in a book for your editing or proofreading, there will be mistakes in the book.'

FRANKENSTEIN

≈ (1818) ≈

'THE SEASON WAS COLD and rainy, and in the evenings we crowded around a blazing wood fire, and occasionally amused ourselves with some German stories of ghosts, which happened to fall into our hands.' So wrote a nineteenth-century author in the preface to a novel which has the subtitle of 'A Modern Prometheus'. The group huddling round the blazing wood fire were far from being the gentleman members of some London club diverting themselves during a winter evening, but rather a hotch-potch of romantic exiles and runaways occupying a rented villa on the edge of Lake Geneva. And it was the middle of summer.*

---

* For much of the northern hemisphere, 1816 was the year of two winters. In Britain

The author by the fire was Mary Shelley, a woman whose life was steeped in literature and radicalism from the beginning. Her mother was Mary Wollstonecraft, an early exponent of women's rights, while her father, William Godwin, was a philosopher and writer with views which would still be called progressive today. In 1814, at the age of 17, Mary Godwin eloped with the poet Percy Shelley, and during the summer of 1816 they joined the group staying at the Villa Diodati by Lake Geneva. Other members included Lord Byron and his mistress of the moment, Claire Clairmont, who happened to be Mary's stepsister, and also the intriguing figure of John Polidori,* usually described as Byron's physician but in reality more of a hanger-on. To a proposal by Byron that they should each come up with a ghost story to while away the wet weather, the response of Mary Godwin – she and Percy Shelley did

---

and western Europe almost continual rain from summer to autumn caused widespread crop failure, while on the other side of the Atlantic the snow which fell in the St Lawrence area on 8 June was deep enough to bury carriages up to their axle-trees. The cause was the eruption of Mount Tambora (on what is now the Indonesian island of Sumbawa), which blew up with approximately four times the energy of the 1883 self-destruction of the better-known Krakatoa, and threw eleven cubic miles of pulverized, floating material into the air. The detritus from this volcanic eruption and two lesser ones elsewhere reflected enough of the sun heat's away from the earth to lower the average temperature in the northern hemisphere by several degrees fahrenheit. Few people other than those in the immediate Pacific region knew anything of the 1815 Tambora eruption.

* John Polidori's contribution to the ghost-story challenge was a novella called 'The Vampyre'. It's not very good but it has the distinction of being the first real vampire story in English.

not marry until the end of 1816 – was the invention of one of the most enduring and ambiguous figures in literature.

Mary Shelley's Geneva-born book was *Frankenstein*, the story of a scientist who creates an artificial being from body-parts that are stolen from graves, put together and then brought to life. The result can be viewed as either human being or monster – or both at the same time. This being is often (and wrongly) called **Frankenstein**, although the creature is never given a name in the novel. When Victor **Frankenstein**, the god-like creator, turns away in horror from what he has constructed and the creature finds himself similarly loathed and rejected by all he meets, he takes revenge on his tormented parent before disappearing into the arctic night to destroy himself. To the very end, the creature has more self-knowledge than the man who made him and is capable of eloquent insights with which Mary's father, the liberal philosopher William Godwin, would have agreed: 'Everywhere I see bliss, from which I alone am irrevocably excluded. I was benevolent and good; misery made me a fiend.'

As a novel *Frankenstein*, first published in 1818, keeps shifting shape: is it a straightforward Gothic horror story, or a disturbing parable of parenthood, or an allegory of the creative process, or a warning about uncontrolled tampering with nature? Unsurprisingly, the title word crops up in this last application in contemporary reports about cloning, designer babies, GM foods and so on. The character and story are easily parodied or travestied, as in Mel Brooks's *Young Frankenstein* or Dr Frank N. Furter in *The Rocky Horror Show*. There's plenty of life yet in **Frankenstein**, whether as story, word or warning.

PASTA

≈ (1830) ≈

I
N 1950S BRITAIN THERE were only two television channels, the BBC and ITV, transmitting for a few hours
each evening and to be viewed on a bulbous screen
encased in a wooden cube set in the corner of the lounge.
One of the most respected of the BBC programmes was
(and still is) *Panorama*, a serious-minded magazine-style
survey of what was then called 'current affairs'. It attracted
audiences of between eight and ten million, a number
greater than anything attained today by *Downton Abbey*
or *Strictly Come Dancing*. Even more respected than *Panorama* was its presenter Richard Dimbleby, father of David
and Jonathan, and a man with, it was said, 'enough gravitas
to float an aircraft carrier'. So when on a Monday evening
in April 1957, Dimbleby announced a final report from the

Swiss Alps, and the scene shifted to idyllic shots of spring blossoms on the shores of Lake Lugano, the audience must have settled back with a mixture of curiosity and perhaps – in a Britain only recently emerging from post-war rationing and the Suez crisis of 1956 – a touch of envy at an easier, more pleasurable way of life on the 'continent'.

Over shots of women picking a string-like crop from trees and laying out the strands to dry in the sun, Dimbleby's reassuring voice-over informed millions of British viewers that: 'The last two weeks of March are an anxious time for the spaghetti farmer. There is always the chance of a late frost [...] But now these dangers are over and the spaghetti harvest goes forward.' Keeping the oral equivalent of a straight face, he continued: 'Spaghetti cultivation here in Switzerland is not, of course, carried out on anything like the tremendous scale of the Italian industry. Many of you, I am sure, will have seen pictures of the vast spaghetti plantations in the Po valley. For the Swiss, however, it tends to be more of a family affair.' And so the report went on in creative detail, stressing how the prospects of a bumper year for spaghetti had been enhanced by the disappearance of the 'spaghetti weevil', and how it had taken years of careful breeding to ensure that the spaghetti produced by the trees was of identical length.

No one knows how many people were fooled by 'the great spaghetti harvest hoax', broadcast on 1 April 1957, though among them was the then director-general of the BBC. (The whole *Panorama* sequence can be viewed on YouTube 'BBC: Spaghetti-Harvest in Ticino'.) Hundreds of viewers phoned in to settle arguments that had broken out in their families: was it really true that spaghetti grew on trees? Others wanted to know how to grow a tree for themselves; the BBC phone operators eventually came up with this formula: 'Place a sprig of spaghetti in a tin of tomato and hope for the best.' Three factors contributed to the success of the hoax: the reputation of the programme and its presenter, the skill of the three-minute sequence, and the fact that many people had only a hazy idea of exactly what spaghetti was or where it came from. Generally sold in tins, it was regarded an exotic delicacy in the United Kingdom.

Perhaps nothing more illustrates the cultural revolution that has overtaken British life – not even the replacement of the twelve-inch goggle-box by the giant flat-screen TV – than the plethora of types of **pasta** now available from the smallest deli to the biggest hypermarket. The word is a direct borrowing from Italian (*pasta*: 'paste, dough'), and is first found in English in 1830. For the record, it does not grow on trees but is a dough made from wheat and water, sometimes enriched with egg. There are dozens of different types of **pasta**, from spaghetti (*spaghetto*: 'thin string') to rigatoni (thick, fluted tubes deriving from *riga*: 'line'), from orecchiette ('little ears') to linguine ('little tongues'), from tagliatelle (*tagliare*: 'to cut') to vermicelli ('little worms'). Most of these words have been in English for a long time, vermicelli and macaroni (also with the meaning of 'dandy') since the seventeenth century, but they have largely been the property of travel writers or cookery writers. It's only in the last forty or so years that they've become public property.

Foodies will be especially concerned with the cooking time of the **pasta**: the preferred result is that it should be *al dente* (literally, 'to the tooth'), tender but retaining a bit of bite. The pungent sauce called 'puttanesca' which often accompanies **pasta** takes its name from the Italian for 'sluttish' or 'characteristic of a prostitute' (*puttana*: prostitute). It is not an insult, but the reasons for the name are obscure. One explanation has a restaurateur on the island of Ischia explaining to hungry customers that he didn't have enough ingredients to make a meal and getting the reply: then just make us a '*puttanata qualsiasi*' or 'any old rubbish' (as with the French *putain* ('prostitute'), prostitute-related terms can be used as swear words, part of disparaging expressions, etc.) Delia Smith calls the result 'tart's spaghetti'. Food writer Felicity Cloake suggests that it originated as a cheap dish which the working girls of Naples could cobble together between turning tricks. And Nigel Slater tells us that the ideal puttanesca sauce should be 'salty', 'piquant', 'hot' and 'coarse'. I think we get the idea.

Quite a few Italian food-related terms have established themselves in English. Minestrone, the thick soup which is a meal in itself, ultimately goes back to an Italian verb meaning 'to serve at table', 'dish out'. The pizza, a word of uncertain origin, is described in an early Victorian guidebook as 'a popular cake [...] not disdained by the higher classes'. Bruschetta is first mentioned in a book by Elizabeth David, who did so much to introduce a grey post-war Britain to more colourful European food and cuisine; crostini similarly date from the 1950s. Carpaccio, for wafer-thin slices of raw beef and, sometimes, of tuna was apparently first created in 1961 in Harry's Bar in Venice, the name inspired by Vittore Carpaccio, a Venetian Renaissance painter who used a distinctive rare-beef, reddish hue in his work. Yet, again according Nigel Slater, 'with its haphazard zigzags and drizzles of its signature sauce, your lunch actually looks much more like a Jackson Pollock'.

The same iconic Venetian bar is said to have produced the Bellini cocktail (peach juice with prosecco or champagne), after an exhibition in the city of work by the fifteenth-century painter, Giovanni Bellini. Prosecco itself is named after a town near Trieste. Also in popular use is antipasto (literally 'before the meal'; *pasto* as in 'repast'); the French equivalent is *hors d'oeuvres*; the best that British English can come up with is 'starters'.

Finally, a handful of linguistic peculiarities from Italy are worth noting. Gnocchi, the little dumplings made with flour or semolina or potato, are named for their shape rather than, one hopes, their texture: in Italian *nocchio* is a knot or knob in wood. (The name of the wooden puppet Pinnochio, whose nose grows longer when he lies, derives not from this but is a diminutive form of *pinolo*: 'pine seed'). The combination of eggs, sugar, mascarpone and coffee-saturated lady's fingers which goes into tiramisu swept the pudding world in the 1980s and later. Tiramisu, which does not appear in dictionaries before that date, means literally 'pick me up', 'pull me up', referring to the restorative effect of the slug of *espresso* which goes into the dish. The word 'marscapone' for the soft creamy cheese which is an essential part of the tiramisu may – only *may* – derive from an old and putative Italian/Latin word for 'take in hand' (i.e. masturbate). For comparison, the *OED* refers to a southern Italian phrase *far ricotta* for 'masturbate' (literally, 'to make *ricotta*'). After that, it is something of a relief to discover that *ricotta* (the cheese) means, in effect, no more than 'recooked'.

BOWDLERIZE

≈ (1836) ≈

THOMAS BOWDLER, WHO WAS born in 1754 to a wealthy family near Bath and trained as a doctor, remembered hearing his father read passages from Shakespeare to the family when he was a child. What he didn't know at the time was that his father was censoring the Shakespeare because 'those matchless tragedies contained words and expressions improper to be pronounced'. These would include oaths and swearing, as well as suggestive puns and sexual innuendo. From the perspective of the time, Bowdler Senior was doing no more than any responsible, respectable father would do. It occurred to Thomas Bowdler that what his father had achieved for his own family, he might do for the wider reading and listening public. The business of cleaning up the world's greatest dramatist, which built on earlier work done by Bowdler's sister Henrietta, resulted in the 1818 publication of *The Family Shakespeare*. Bowdler explained that, while nothing had been added to the text, 'those words and expressions are omitted which cannot with propriety be read aloud in a family'. The book became a bestseller and went through several editions. At the time of his death in 1825 Bowdler had just completed a revised edition of Edward Gibbon's *History of the Decline and Fall of the Roman Empire*, which left out 'all passages of an irreligious or immoral tendency'.

From the beginning, and despite the high sales of *The Family Shakespeare*, Bowdler's project attracted suspicion and even ridicule. The verb **bowdlerize**, first cited in 1836 and meaning to 'expurgate a text so that anything offensive is removed', was never meant as a compliment. Even so, Bowdler has been defended on the grounds that his cuts to Shakespeare were fairly minor, that he never added anything to the text, and that he did at least make the plays accessible to 'intelligent and imaginative children'. The spirit of Bowdler lived on for well over a century. When I was doing English O Level in the mid-1960s, and we were studying the *Prologue* to Chaucer's *The Canterbury Tales*, a line describing the Pardoner was marked only by a series of dots. The inflammatory line comes after a description of the Pardoner's smooth but unshaven cheeks and casts doubt on his sexuality or gender. In full, it reads: '*I trowe* [believe] *he were a gelding or a mare.'* Too dangerous to be read by fifteen-year-olds, evidently.

Bowdlerize is an example of an eponymous verb, that is, one formed from a proper name. In their very nature, such terms tend to describe practices or processes that didn't exist or at least had no specific name before the inventor/innovator came along. By this method several verbs have been added to the English language including galvanize (from Luigi Galvani), guillotine (Joseph-Ignace Guillotin), pasteurize (Louis Pasteur), mesmerize (Friedrich Anton Mesmer), boycott (from Captain Boycott, a land agent on an Irish estate in the nineteenth century), lynch (from Lynch Law, and originating with either a Charles or a William Lynch in the US), gerrymander* and Mirandize (in the US, to inform an arrested suspect of his rights, including the key right to remain silent, and so named after a Supreme Court case involving one Ernesto Miranda).

---

* The Democrat Governor of Massachusetts, Elbridge Gerry, signed a bill in 1812 redrawing district boundaries to favour his own party and weaken the opposition. When a Boston newspaper artist added a head, wings and claws to the unnaturally redrawn map and said it looked like a salamander, his editor exclaimed, 'Salamander! Call it a Gerrymander!'

OK

≈ (1839) ≈

ENGLISH IS THE CLOSEST that the world has come to possessing a universal language, not in the sense that everyone can speak it – the large majority of the world's population cannot – but because most people are likely to be familiar with a handful of English expressions, including a couple of brands (Coke, Manchester United). The oldest and most truly global term is also the shortest: **OK** (or O.K. or okay), originating in America in the nineteenth century. An astonishingly versatile word, it works as almost any part of speech from noun to verb to adjective to adverb, though often just as a conversation-filler – 'OK, what next?' Depending on tone of voice and context, **OK** occupies any position on the spectrum from fervent agreement to mild acquiescence, to a mere acknowledgement that the speaker is listening or simply still alive. The simplicity, snappiness and adaptability of **OK** are the reasons for its success.

It may be appropriate that such a truly universal term has no finally agreed source. Among the theories are: that it comes from the Choctaw Indians or that it was brought across from west Africa or that it derives from French sailors who during the War of Independence made assignations with American women *aux quais* (at the quayside) or that it is a version of the Scotch 'och aye'... and so on. It's a relief to turn to the *Oxford English Dictionary* and find that the first citation comes from a Baltimore newspaper in 1839, where o.k. is identified as a shortened version of 'all correct' (humorously misspelled as 'oll korrekt'). By a happy coincidence, the following year saw the sitting US President Martin Van Buren launch his campaign for re-election. A Democrat, Van Buren came from the village of Kinderhook in upstate New York, and was consequently referred to as Old Kinderhook, or O.K. An O.K. Club in New York campaigned for Van Buren's return to office while a typical rallying-cry went: 'Down with the whigs,* boys, O.K.' The overlapping of popular usage and an election campaign seem to have cemented the word in

---

* The Whig Party was the opposition to the Democrats in the earlier part of the nineteenth century. The Republican Party, or the GOP (Grand Old Party), did not appear until shortly before the Civil War.

American consciousness and it slowly won approval in other English-speaking countries before becoming established as the most popular two letters in the world. Martin Van Buren did not get re-elected but almost certainly he did, indirectly, bequeath us **OK**.

OXBRIDGE

≈ (1849) ≈

AFICIONADOS OF US CRIME fiction and shows may be familiar with the 'chop shop', a place less alarming than it sounds since it involves no grievous bodily harm but the dismembering of a (probably) stolen car or the welding together of two disparate halves to make a 'new' vehicle. Words too can go into the chop shop, when two existing terms are inventively but forcibly pushed into a partnership that neither of them may have expected. In the process, a part of each term will be lost even as something new is gained. As with chopped cars, the result may well be a bit ugly but such words form a small but quite widely used area of modern English.

Oxbridge, an old and relatively smooth example of chopping, was created by William Thackeray in his novel

Pendennis (1849) to describe a university which was neither Oxford nor Cambridge but an imagined institution combining both names. Later the term moved from the purely descriptive to have connotations of elitism and intellectual snobbery. It was the author Lewis Carroll who christened such joined-up terms in *Alice Through the Looking Glass* (1871) when he had Humpty Dumpty explain to Alice the meaning of 'slithy': 'Well, "slithy" means "lithe and slimy." "Lithe" is the same as "active." You see it's like a portmanteau – there are two meanings packed up into one word.' A portmanteau is a smallish case designed to open into two halves. Carroll himself was responsible for a handful of portmanteau terms: chortle ('chuckle' + 'snort'), galumph ('gallop' + 'triumph'), and mimsy ('miserable' + 'flimsy') though this now seems to be used more in the sense of 'twee'.

The examples of portmanteau terms given above sound fairly natural as do long-established items such as brunch ('breakfast' + 'lunch', and originally a piece of Oxbridge slang from the late nineteenth century), motel ('motor' + 'hotel', first cited 1925), Jacobethan (the architectural combination of 'Jacobean' and 'Elizabethan', coined by John Betjeman in 1933), moped ('motor' + 'pedal', 1954), Franglais* (French + English, 1959). The more recent the

---

* Franglais describes a mixture of the two languages, often employing the French definite article, *le*, with an English noun: *le parking, le fun, le planning*. It's easy to see which language comes off worse here. The French – never keen, at an

portmanteau, the more contrived it may sound, perhaps because it sounds less familiar to the ear. Examples, mostly ugly ones, are not difficult to find: Brangelina (Pitt + Jolie), bromance ('bro' + 'romance'), chillax ('chill out' + 'relax'), spork ('spoon' + 'fork'), shwopping ('shopping' + 'swopping' – a marketing initiative to get people to buy new clothes while giving older ones away to charity shops), brinner ('breakfast' + 'dinner', i.e. breakfast eaten at any time of day).

official level, to acknowledge the primacy of English or its global spread – do not welcome English imports into their language, especially if there are already home-grown words apparently doing the same job. Why talk about *le weekend* when you could (and should) be saying *le fin de semaine*? (One answer is that they mean slightly different things: *le weekend* covers Saturday–Sunday while *le fin de semaine* can apply to the last two or three days of the week.) Instead the French might look on the English language as a source of pride since, following on the 1066 conquest, they contributed a great deal more to us than we have ever contributed to them.

NIRVANA

∝ (1864) ∝

NIRVANA IS ONE OF a small group of words from Sanskrit, the ancient language of India, which have Buddhist or Hindu associations and which began to appear in English from the middle of the nineteenth century. They really came into their own in the mystical, psychedelic 1960s, stowed away in the backpacks of returning hippies or travelling home first-class with The Beatles after one of their sessions with the Maharishi ('great seer') Mahesh Yogi. Having the literal meaning of 'extinction' in Sanskrit, **nirvana** signifies in Buddhism the release of the self from the cycle of life and death, and by extension a 'blissful state'. To be in such a state is to be released from the effects of 'karma'. This complex concept is both action and fate, since it embodies the belief that the sum of actions in an individual life, or a series of lives, determines status or fate in the next incarnation; under karma, fate is not an impersonal, externally imposed destiny but something which, to an extent, is self-chosen. To guide one through this belief system, one might well need the help of a 'guru' or teacher, a 'pundit' or learned man (*pandita*: Sanskrit), a *swami* or master/religious teacher, and a *yogi* (a practitioner of yoga, the system which combines asceticism and meditation for spiritual purposes). Any of these guides and teachers might instruct one in the importance of the 'mantra' ('thought': Sanskrit), a sacred word or phrase to be repeated in prayer or incantation.

Unsurprisingly, most of these terms, once in contact with Western culture, largely lose their religious or sacred significance. A trace of their origins may still cling to them, however, imparting a pseudo-spiritual or mystical note. **Nirvana**, when it doesn't refer to Kurt Cobain's outfit, often equates to a holiday heaven, an expensive upmarket destination. Karma is reduced in general use to not much more than the notion of cause-and-effect, swings-and-roundabouts, what-goes-around-comes-around. At its most reductive, the word is the verbal equivalent of shrugging the shoulders ('It's *karma*, man'). The *guru* had his heyday in the 1960s but the word is still widely used to denote a teacher/expert – even if it occasionally suggests one who gives himself airs – while pundit, more of an expert than a teacher, is a fairly neutral term, quite often connected to political commentary. The US has the verb form of 'punditize'. The 'mantra', meanwhile, indicates a belief or idea which can be encapsulated in a few words and which, most probably, goes unexamined ('In the first speech by a Prime Minister on prisons in more than two decades he will roundly reject the old Tory hang 'em and flog 'em mantra of previous leaders ...' *Independent*).

JEHAD

❧ (1869) ❧

T HE GENERAL DEFINITION OF **jehad** is 'holy war', and specifically one of Muslims against non-believers. Now spelled *jihad* and, along with its offshoots *jihadi* and *jihadist*, grimly familiar in the Western media, the word derives from the Arabic term for 'striving' or 'contest', especially in relation to the spread of Islam. It can refer to an inner spiritual struggle but its almost universal application now is to external struggle, usually interpreted as war, whether covert or overt. The term may have been ubiquitous since the September 11 attacks in New York, but it's hardly new. The idea of jihad is at the root of John Buchan's adventure thriller, *Greenmantle* (1916), which dramatizes – or melodramatizes – the German attempt to use its alliance with Turkey during the First World War to provoke an uprising against the infidel West. In Buchan's romantic vision, the then colonial lands of the Middle East were only waiting for a leader and prophet to spearhead a jihad: 'There is a dry wind blowing through the East, and the parched grasses wait the spark,' says the intelligence chief Sir Walter Bullivant, while another character remarks: 'You never know what will start off a jehad!' The subject of Islam and *jihad* was and is so sensitive that a radio dramatization of *Greenmantle*, scheduled to be broadcast in July 2005, was postponed because of the London bombings in that month.

Ever since it resurfaced at the start of a new millennium, jihad has been used from time to time to suggest any supposedly fanatical drive or campaign in a non-Islamist context. It's a convenient piece of partisan ammunition, whether from the right, 'For the current jihad against hunting cannot be viewed in isolation from the other injustices being visited on non-metropolitan Britain' (on Tony Blair's government, *The Times*); or the left, 'Ever since the Thatcher era [...] the Tories have pursued a jihad against local government ... ' (*New Statesman*, of David Cameron's government).

AGORAPHOBIA

≈ (1871) ≈

T HERE IS A LITERAL A–Z of hundreds of phobias, from acrophobia (fear of heights) to zoophobia (fear of animals), all of them characterizing a state of extreme anxiety provoked by an object or situation, and which though possibly containing an element of sense is largely irrational. 'Phobia' and the adjectival 'phobic' can stand by themselves as words but since it is easy to use them in compound forms ('needle phobia', 'festive phobia', 'school phobia') or to attach them as suffixes to almost anything ('technophobic', 'Europhobic', 'pogonophobic'*) there can

---

* Literally 'fearful of beards'. According to Michael Quinion on his *World Wide Words* website, the word is not to be found before the 1980s and, like its noun cousin 'pogonophobia', should not be taken too seriously either. The word achieved a brief fame in 2013 when presenter Jeremy Paxman returned to BBC2's

be a do-it-yourself quality to some of the linguistic coinages. 'Hydrophobia', first recorded in the early seventeenth century, seems to be the first such formation. There are a few -phobias found in the next century although 'aversion' or some equivalent term was more usual. The great phobic wave comes, unsurprisingly, in the nineteenth century with the rising interest in psychology and the classification of human behaviour and its aberrations.

Agoraphobia comes initially from German (*Agoraphobie*) but is a combination of two ancient Greek words, *agora* ('open space'; 'marketplace') and *phobos* ('fear'). As the derivation suggests, it can describe a dread not just of open spaces but of crowded ones too. The opposite dread of 'claustrophobia' joins a Latin term *claustrum* ('closed space', as in 'cloister') with the same Greek suffix. The existence of an ancient Greek hook on which to hang various psychological or other conditions means that the preceding word, the thing that defines the phobia, is likely to appear in a Greek or Latinate form too. Conditions may be doubly named: the fear of water or inability to swallow, which is a symptom of rabies and is known as 'hydrophobia' (Greek, ὕδωρ/*hydor*: 'water') may also be called 'aquaphobia' (Latin, *aqua*: 'water').

Newsnight wearing a beard after his summer holidays. This caused more of a stir than anything actually in the news and Paxman commented that 'the BBC is generally as pogonophobic as the late-lamented Albanian dictator, Enver Hoxha'.

BULLDOZER

❦ (1876) ❧

T HIS IS ONE OF those words whose origins are more sinister than current use suggests. A **bulldozer** now is either the construction machine, a literal earth-mover, or is applied metaphorically to a person who gets their own way by battering down opposition. But in its alternative spelling of 'bull-doser' (i.e. one who administers a dose fit for a bull) it most likely signified someone who meted out a brutal flogging to a black person in the American South. Early uses of 'bull-dose/doze' point to the intimidation and persecution which continued after the end of the American Civil War in 1865. Other references in the 1870s and '80s link the **bulldozer** to thuggish or mob-like behaviour in general, and the word was also applied to a Californian gun that fired a bullet 'heavy enough to destroy human life with certainty'. There may be a more general link with the bull-whip, the long-lashed whip used on cattle-drives.

A small handful of other terms emerged in the aftermath of the Civil War. A 'carpet-bagger' was an individual from the North who took advantage of the political and economic Reconstruction of the South and who fulfilled a 'property qualification' with the contents of the carpet-bag – i.e. a bag made of carpet-like material – he brought with him. In the US today the term is still applied pejoratively to a politician who moves to another state with the intention of seeking political office there. (The British equivalent is a 'parachute candidate', one dropped in from the outside and with little real knowledge of the constituency he or she is going to stand for.) The origin of the next word is unknown but the 'scallywag' was a disreputable individual, one from the South who was willing to work with the victorious Yankees in the Reconstruction and, in effect, a turncoat or collaborator. A 'cakewalk' was a contest of black American walking/dancing which may have started in mockery of the strutting white way of moving. The prize was – a cake. By the end of the nineteenth century cakewalk came to signify something easy, in which sense it still remains. In 2002, before the ousting of Saddam Hussein, a member of the Pentagon's Policy Board claimed that 'liberating Iraq would be a cakewalk', one of many predictions which came back to haunt the administration of George W. Bush.

DOPPELGÄNGER

≈ (1879) ≈

THE GERMAN WORD *DOPPELGÄNGER*, literally meaning a double-goer, makes its earliest appearance in English in the form of 'double-ganger' in 1830 in a book by Walter Scott on demonology. It's appropriate that a word to do with doubles should exist in two shapes – or three if you count the variant spelling of *doppleganger* – and also appropriate that it emerges in the Victorian era. This was a period curiously concerned with doubles, wraiths and fetches, as they were sometimes called. In the twenty-first century meeting your **doppelgänger**** seems a reason to celebrate ('Priest greeted by

---

*   The *umlaut* in doppelgänger, the double dots over the 'a', indicates how the third vowel should be pronounced. The *umlaut* (German: literally 'around' + 'sound') only appears in English when words from Germanic languages are being used.

strangers discovers doppelganger neighbour', *Daily Telegraph* headline) and there's even a website called Twin Strangers to help you do it. You select your facial features, find others with the same profile, and hook up. But to encounter your double in the nineteenth century was a more sinister affair, as attested by a variety of stories from James Hogg's peculiar cult novel *The Private Memoirs and Confessions of a Justified Sinner* (1824) through Robert Louis Stevenson's *Dr Jekyll and Mr Hyde* (1886) to Joseph Conrad's *The Secret Sharer* (1910). The first two are literary examples of the Gothic, a word which points to the beating Germanic heart of narratives haunted by spectres, wraiths and poltergeists ('rumbling ghost': German).

The debt of English to old Germanic words is incalculable, since in mutated form they provide the bedrock of Old English. But direct imports from modern German into English are fairly few in number. Perhaps the number-one import is *schadenfreude*, or 'pleasure in the misfortune

---

The Icelandic singer Björk is one example. Two others are Führer, meaning 'leader' but in practice restricted to Hitler, and (Hermann) Göring. An idea of the pronunciation change produced by the double dots is shown by the alternative spellings of Fuehrer and Goering. Heavy metal bands like Motörhead and Mötley Crüe use the umlaut in their spellings. It's no guide to pronunciation but it looks hard, heavy and Teutonic. The mark has a curious appeal in branding: the now defunct Möben Kitchens operated under the umlaut, even though the name came from founders called Mo and Ben, while the puddings company Gü adopted their Germanic-sounding name after toying with French *goût* or 'taste' before realizing it might be confused with that painful condition, gout.

or embarrassment of others', a word which the English regard as a long-lost friend judging by the frequency with which they use it. A related word, and one that like *schadenfreude* doesn't reflect very well on the person feeling it, is the lesser known *Erfolgsneid* or envy/displeasure at a friend's success.* Occupying other positions in the Anglo-German top ten, or at least in the top twenty, are: *kaput* ('finished', 'clapped-out'), *wunderkind* (literally 'wonder-child' but usually applied to anyone who's very successful early in life), *zeitgeist* ('spirit of the age', but sometimes used in English in the adjectival and unGermanic form of zeit-geisty: 'trendy'), *diktat* ('a rule which can't be disputed'), *-fest*, used as a suffix but rarely in a serious context (gab-fest, campfest, bonkfest), *ersatz* (literally 'compensation' or 'replacement' but in English usually applying to an inferior substitute, as 'ersatz coffee'), *spiel* ('talk') and *verboten* ('forbidden'). There's a slightly humorous quality to some of these terms, or rather to the manner in which an English speaker will use, say, *verboten* or *kaput*.

Other expressions hint at the high seriousness of German culture. Words such as *Weltanschauung* ('individual or group world view') or *Weltschmerz* (literally 'world-pain' and so 'pessimism or sadness') or *Gestalt* ('shape or form',

---

* Gore Vidal said: 'Every time a friend succeeds, I die a little.' A fine example of *Erfolgsneid* and used as the title of a biography of the US writer, wit and critic published in 2015.

in the sense of a totality) don't often appear in English, and when they do are signalled as foreign by being italicized or by the use of the Germanic noun capital. But the very fact that they do appear in English in the first place suggests there is a need for them, even if it is an infrequent one.

BALACLAVA

≈ (1881) ≈

T HE **BALACLAVA**, A PIECE of headgear designed to leave only part of the face exposed, took its name from the woollen coverings sent out to British troops during the Crimean War and worn by them as protection against bitter cold. Named after the Crimean village of Balaclava near Sebastopol where the battle involving the Charge of the Light Brigade took place in 1854, the term **balaclava** – helmet or hat – took several years to catch on.

Balaclava is one of many examples of an item of clothing or a piece of kit being awarded an eponymous name. There seem to be several sources for this particular branch of nomenclature: things may be named either for the place where they were manufactured (jeans, originally from a cloth manufactured in medieval Genoa; jersey, from the

Channel Island of the same name), or from a material used (as in Harris tweed), or after an individual involved in their creation or manufacture (Burberry), or because of someone famous associated with the item, as with the Mae West lifejacket. This is a subject which requires a whole book in itself, and there is space here to cover only a handful of such names. In fact, far from going from head to toe, I am going to restrict myself to heads and feet, and then only to expressions from the nineteenth and twentieth centuries.

Several headgear names merely indicate their place of origin, either specifically or regionally: homburg (from the German spa town of Bad Homburg), fez (from either Turkey or Morocco), panama, tyrolean. The word 'millinery' itself comes originally from Milan in northern Italy, where milliners sold fancy items of apparel, and in particular hats. It is a feature of some hats whose names derive from individuals that they tend to have thoroughly up-market origins. The stylish black homburg worn by Anthony Eden, the British Foreign Secretary during the Second World War, was known in Savile Row simply as the 'Eden'. A century earlier, the bowler was reputedly designed by London hat-makers Thomas and William Bowler after a commission from a member of the Coke family, then as now the owners of Holkham Hall in Norfolk. The brief was to create a tough piece of headgear for the estate's gamekeepers to protect their heads from low-hanging branches when out riding. The St James's hatters, Lock & Co, still advertise a 'Town Coke' and an 'Extra-firm Coke'. The bowler was so traditional a part of a gentleman's outfit that, for the officer class after both world wars, to be 'given one's bowler hat' was to make one's return from military to civilian life. In the US the equivalent hat is known as a derby, even if the name derives from the opposite side of the Atlantic: they are probably called after the style of hat worn at the famous Derby races held at Epsom Downs in Surrey, which in turn get their name from the founder of the races, the twelfth earl of Derby. The high-crowned, broad-brimmed stetson takes its name from the Philadelphia manufacturer, founded by John B. Stetson in the nineteenth century. That other staple of Wild West millinery, the ten-gallon hat, is a misnomer (see under **Barbecue**, page 187).

The soft felt hat known as the fedora comes from *Fédora*, the title of an 1882 drama in which Sarah Bernhardt played Princess Fédora Romanoff. *Brewer's Dictionary of Phrase and Fable* saves the trouble of any further investigation into the play by calling it 'preposterous'. It's not clear whether Bernhardt wore such a hat in the production, or whether the name simply struck a fashionable chord with manufacturers and advertisers. (There is also an 1883 reference to a 'Fedora redingote', the Frenchified version of 'riding coat'.) Another soft felt hat with a literary pedigree is the trilby, from the novel of the same name by George du Maurier. Though largely forgotten and certainly unread now, *Trilby** (1894) was a roaring success in its day, to the extent that everything about it was pored over, discussed and imitated. Du Maurier was a cartoonist rather than a novelist, and produced his own illustrations – there are 121 of them – for the book. One of them depicts a character called Little Billee wearing a particular type of soft hat which, in the words of a newspaper report, 'has been seized upon by those worshippers at the shrine of Trilby'. Hence the trilby, discovered on a man's head but named for the heroine. The eponym was also used for a style of shoe in the US. Another item of literary headwear comes from Robert Burns's poem 'Tam o'Shanter',[†] the name of his character and then the term for the round, flat-topped circular cap once worn by Scottish ploughmen and still an item of military wear.

---

*   *Trilby* also introduced Svengali into the English language. A sinister character, Svengali is a musician and a mesmerist who turns Trilby, an artist's model, into a great singer before marrying her. After he dies, her talent fades. Hence we have the expression 'Svengali-like' to characterize any manipulative (and usually male) attempt to control someone else's life and career. George du Maurier, the grandfather of Daphne du Maurier, was a close friend of Henry James, who was baffled by – and envious of – the enormous popular success of *Trilby* compared to the reception and sales of his own much more subtle work. The James–du Maurier friendship is at the core of David Lodge's excellent novel *Author, Author* (2004).

†   Burns's 'Tam o'Shanter' also gives us the Scottish 'cutty sark' or 'short shirt/nightshirt'. Visitors to the *Cutty Sark*, the tea clipper which is in dry dock in Greenwich and named after the garment, will see the painting in which Tam is pursued on horseback by a witch in a very short, see-through nightie.

The world of shoes is not quite so richly eponymous or curious as that of the hat. Leaving aside the high-end designer brands like Jimmy Choo and Manolo Blahnik, there are a handful of shoe types named for places or deriving from people. The Oxford (shoe), now describing an ordinary lace-up and first cited in 1847, most likely derives from the university and may refer to the lighter footwear popular with students who were turning against the more traditional boots of the time. The Wellington boot comes from the Iron Duke and the style of boot that he wore, even if the first written occurrence in 1813, two years before the battle of Waterloo, refers to 'Wellington half-boots'. The Wellington was named after a man who later became prime minister but the boot was on the other foot, so to speak, when Winston Churchill borrowed a name *from* his shoemakers while travelling to summit conferences during the Second World War. For security reasons Churchill was denoted by an assumed name, and he obviously enjoyed picking and varying his own pseudonyms. Among them were Colonel Warden, Mr Kent (perhaps in allusion to his country home at Chertwell) and Mr Lobb, after John Lobb, the still-thriving London company which made the prime minister's shoes.

Less familiar shoes in the UK, and deriving at the turn of the twentieth century from a character in a US comic strip, are Mary Janes, low single-strapped shoes associated with childhood but also wearable by adults. Adidas and Dr Martens (often Docs or DMs in the UK) are both German in origin and named from founders who set up their companies soon after the end of the Second World War, Adi Dassler and Klaus Märtens. The American Nike brand is named after the Greek goddess of victory.

BOOBY-PRIZE

⊰ (1889) ⊱

'BOOBY' HAS BEEN USED as a disparaging term for a man who is slow, stupid and lumbering since at least the beginning of the seventeenth century. As Dr Johnson said in his 1755 *Dictionary*, it is 'a word of no certain etymology', though that didn't stop him attacking an earlier writer, Thomas 'Henshaw [who] thinks it a corruption of *bull-beef* ridiculously'. But Johnson also speculated that it might derive from the Spanish *bobo* ('stupid'), and this is now the generally accepted derivation. The shortened form of 'boob',* meaning a nincompoop, appears at the start of the twentieth century.

---

* Boob/booby/boobies as twentieth-century slang for a woman's breasts is unrelated to the male-related sense of 'idiot', and is a variant on the much older bubby/bubbies.

Booby-prize is first mentioned in 1889 in *Puck*, a New York satirical magazine, to describe a derisory award made to the last/slowest/least competent person in some contest.

Another booby-related term is 'boob', in the sense of a clumsy mistake, because that's the kind of thing a booby does. Then there's the familiar booby-trap as well as the less well-known booby-hutch (for a small cart and perhaps so-called because it was clumsy and lumbering; also a prison-cell) and booby-hatch. This last was US slang for a prison or a lunatic asylum. (The slow and childlike Lennie in John Steinbeck's *Of Mice and Men* [1937] is teased and bullied by others in the ranch-house: 'Want me ta tell ya what'll happen? They'll take ya to the booby hatch. They'll tie ya up with a collar, like a dog.') Interestingly, there may be a link between the slang term 'booby-hatch' and an actual asylum, built in the grand Italianate-Victorian style and now converted to private apartments, in the Colney Hatch district of the north London borough of Barnet. Colney Hatch, later the Friern Mental Hospital, was founded in 1853 and did not close until 1993. It was the largest asylum in Europe, and references in the early twentieth century by writers such as G. K. Chesterton and C. S. Lewis show that the institution and its function were well known.

CHUTZPAH

⁓ (1892) ⁓

THERE'S AN OLD HUMOROUS definition of the Yiddish word **chutzpah** which refers to the son who kills his mother and father and, when found guilty, asks the court for leniency on the grounds that he is an orphan. **Chutzpah** is cheek or brazenness, but the word has an elusive nuance that distinguishes it from those two English synonyms, and this sense of something extra is very characteristic of Yiddish. The first citation of the word comes from *Children of the Ghetto* by Israel Zangwill (also the author of a classic locked-room puzzle, *The Big Bow Mystery*).

Yiddish derives in part from a form of German which Jewish settlers picked up in the Rhineland a thousand years ago, although uniquely it's a European language rendered in Hebrew script. (It is not the same as Hebrew, now the official language of Israel as well as the one used for prayer and ritual, even if Yiddish does contain some Hebrew words.) Leo Rosten points out in *The New Joys of Yiddish* (2001) that Jewish women, because they were not taught the 'sacred tongue' (Hebrew), instead used Yiddish to talk to their children with the consequence that 'Yiddish became known as *mameloshn*, "mother tongue"'. It may have been the language of the ghetto but it also became the *lingua franca* of Jews across central Europe. As a result you can't really say where Yiddish is *from*, since it has a transnational quality. This makes it an especially appropriate contribution to the linguistic treasure-house of the United States, which might be described as the ultimate transnational nation. In the decades before the First World War, an estimated three million Jews from eastern and central Europe, escaping persecution or looking for a better life, entered the US via the immigration centre on New York's Ellis Island. They may not have been carrying much luggage but, like other immigrants, they brought energy and creativity – and their own language. So prevalent was it that as late as 1935 New Yorkers could choose between a dozen Yiddish newspapers.

The choice was not restricted to newspapers. Yiddish is rich in terms that combine amusement and disdain. The sound alone is almost enough to convey the meaning of *schmuck*, *putz* and *klutz*, all three suggesting fools, with the first two being slang terms for penis and the third coming from a Germanic word meaning 'wooden block'. Other, slightly more rarefied Yiddish terms like *nebbish* ('hapless person') or *schlemiel* ('fool') or *schnorrer* ('whinging beggar') are not so familiar. Yet more such terms than one might expect are in, or on the edges of, popular usage, especially in the metropolitan centres of the United States. One reason is the (originally immigrant) Jewish contribution to the film and popular music businesses over more than a century, something whose significance and value can hardly be overestimated. Another related reason is the cultural impact of American writers like Philip Roth and Joseph Heller. Apart from Howard Jacobson, it is hard to find any equivalent figures in British literature. Or (as it would be phrased Yiddish-style): in Britain, not so much.

Nevertheless quite a few Yiddish expressions have found a place in mainstream British English and some like 'nosh' (originally 'nash') and 'kitsch' are of longstanding. Phrases like 'Go figure' or 'Enough already', perhaps more familiar in the States, are further examples of Yiddish-influenced English. But while a handful of words are obvious enough in their application – glitch, bagel – many retain a slightly exotic tinge and are not always easy to 'translate'. Take *schlep*, first cited in James Joyce's *Ulysses* (1922), in which the author helpfully provides his own gloss on the meaning: 'She trudges, schlepps, trains, drags, trascines* her load.' So we can glean that *schle(p) ping* is a tiresome process, something long and laborious and probably involving much pulling and tugging over a distance. But the Yiddish word is more expressive than its English equivalents, with an almost onomatopoeic quality, the sound of one weary foot after another connecting with the pavement and being dragged along it. Yet that doesn't quite capture the essence of *schlep* either. Things are complicated by the existence of the word *schlepper*, with the sense, like so many Yiddish words, of 'fool' or 'scrounger'. So, does it take a schlepper to schlep properly? Other Yiddish terms are tricky too: *maven* ('an expert', but with the merest suggestion of 'self-proclaimed'), *schmaltzy* ('sentimental to the point of being sickly' – derives from the German word for cooking fat), *schmooze* ('chatter/network'), *shtum* ('silent, dumb', but only about things which it would be compromising or risky to reveal). Yes, Yiddish is hard to put into other words.

---

* Of course, 'trascines' is nothing to do with Yiddish but what's called a nonce-word, i.e. a word made up for the occasion and not found anywhere else. James Joyce, a dab hand at nonce-words, derived this particular one from the Italian for drag or pull (*trascinare*). Joyce's invention of quark (see page 317) would have remained a nonce-word had it not been taken up later to describe an atomic particle. And it should be noted that this sense of nonce is unconnected with the much later, slang sense of the word to describe a sex offender, usually against children. That nonce comes probably from 'nance' or a dialect term signifying a good-for-nothing.

KAMIKAZE

❧ (1896) ❧

WHEN IN 1588 A storm scattered the Spanish Armada launched against the England of Elizabeth I by Catholic Spain, a thankful nation referred to it as the Protestant Wind. A similar response – that providence rather than nature should be thanked if your country is protected by the elements – had already occurred three centuries earlier and half a world away. Typhoons destroyed two Mongol invasion fleets sent against Japan by Kublai Khan in 1274 and 1281, and this salvation-by-storm was referred to as a 'divine wind' or *kami-kaze*. During the Second World War, the Japanese transferred the term to both the pilots and planes which launched suicidal attacks on Allied shipping in the Pacific, particularly the larger targets like carriers and landing craft. Around 5,000 **kamikaze** pilots died in the last ten months of the war before Japan's surrender in August 1945. The same month saw the first citation of **kamikaze** in this new suicidal sense in the US magazine *Newsweek*. Now the term is used, and quite widely, to characterize behaviour which ranges from the suicidal to the merely reckless ('...a kamikaze media reform package which merely picked a fight with the press on the cusp of an election' *Spectator*). The French use the Japanese word to describe a present-day suicide bomber.

Very few expressions from Japanese had penetrated English even by the eighteenth century. The only ones generally recognizable now are *koi* (for the carp), *samurai* ('warrior') defined as someone carrying two swords or sabres, and two terms relating to religious systems, *Shinto* (as Sinto) and *Zen*. It's probably no coincidence that the Japanese terms most familiar to Western ears emerged in the nineteenth century, when both Japan and China were emerging from a long era of isolation. Among these familiar words are: *ju-jitsu*, *sumo* (wrestling), *geisha*, *kimono*, *banzai* (a war cry, literally 'ten thousand years' and originally a greeting to the Japanese emperor), *futon*, *yen* (the coin), *tycoon* (from Japan but ultimately deriving from Chinese for 'great prince'), and *hara-kiri*. This last, describing a ritualistic means of suicide by disembowelling, comes from combining two words, 'belly' and 'cut'. But according to an observer in 1890, quoted in the *OED*, 'The Japanese almost always prefer to employ the synonym *seppuku*, which they consider more elegant because it is derived from the Chinese.'

The last hundred years or so have seen only a handful of Japanese terms come into the language, several of them food-related (*sukiyaki, teriyaki, sushi, tempura, ramen*). *Karaoke* (literally 'empty orchestra') is a recent entrant, as is *umami* to describe a supposed 'fifth taste' which complements the official foursome of salty, sweet, bitter and sour. This is an odd term not so much because it can't be defined – it translates as 'deliciousness' – but because it seems to leave food-writers struggling to pin down its exact nature. According to Heston Blumenthal *umami* was coined by a scientist at Tokyo Imperial University in 1908. Blumenthal characterizes the taste as 'savoury, meaty and broth-like' and says that foods with a naturally high *umami* content include Parmesan, shiitake mushrooms and fermented oriental fish sauce products.

Finally, a couple of Japanese curiosities are worth noting. One is 'honcho', literally a 'squad leader' and so a boss or manager. Generally coupled with 'head' for its alliterative value rather than sense, since a honcho is a head by definition, the term is often assumed to be Spanish/Mexican. (A newspaper ad of some years ago featured a picture of a sombrero'd Mexican with the tag-line 'So you want to be the head honcho?') It isn't Spanish but Japanese. Also oddly popular is 'tsunami', literally 'harbour wave', but in practice 'tidal wave', which is itself a misnomer since it properly refers to high water produced by the tide rather than by an undersea earthquake. Even before the Indian Ocean tsunami of 2004, which caused mass casualties, the Japanese word was often found in English, and it continues to be. While I was writing this paragraph, I checked the *Guardian*'s website and found eleven occurrences of tsunami in the previous three days alone.

DETENTE

∾ (1908) ∾

THERE ARE PLENTY OF French terms that have been imported wholesale and unchanged into Britain and the English-speaking world, and they form a minor but significant stratum of the language. These terms may, incidentally, also throw a light on French tastes and preoccupations, or what are popularly supposed to be the tastes and preoccupations of our oldest neighbours and enemies. Among much else, these imports from across the Channel conjure up a world of cooking (*amuse-bouche, cordon bleu, haute cuisine*), of fashion (*chic, bon ton, haute couture*) and manners (*politesse, noblesse oblige, comme il faut*). Above all, there are expressions connected with love, sex and bodily parts: *poule de luxe, soixante-neuf, billet doux, femme fatale, grande horizontale, mariage blanc, embonpoint, derrière, cinq à sept.** Even *gigolo*, which sounds as though it might have come from Italian, is actually French.

So when it comes to choosing a single word to illustrate a direct French hit upon the English language we're faced with what they might term an *embarras de richesse* or perhaps an *embarras de choix*. In French, **détente**, first appearing in English in *The Times* in 1908, has a primary sense of 'loosening' or 'relaxation', whether of the physical or intellectual kind. But it's the secondary sense that has been exported around the English-speaking world, one that describes an easing of the tensions in (previously poor) relations between countries. The word really came into vogue in the 1970s and '80s as the Cold War between the Communist East and the capitalist West started to thaw. The interesting point here is that **détente** is a political/diplomatic term, and that French has bequeathed us a fair number of such expressions. They include *coup (d'état)*, *regime, bloc, démarche, etiquette, rapprochement, attaché, chargé d'affaires, chef de cabinet, aide* (who might also produce an *aide-mémoire*). Even the collective term for the entirety of all foreign representatives living in a particular

---

* Out of this cornucopia of amorous terms, there is space to touch only on one. *Cinq à sept* (literally, 'five to seven o'clock') is the stretch of time in the late afternoon when lovers enjoy a get-together or a man pops into a brothel on his way home. At least that's how it is or was, reputedly, in France. The elegance and obliquity of French is shown by the English equivalent to *cinq à sept*: 'the naughty pause'.

country – the diplomatic corps – is only a tweaking of the original French expression *le corps diplomatique*.

French has sometimes been called the language of diplomacy, and the reasons are both historical and linguistic. France was the dominant power in western Europe from the time of the Sun King, Louis XIV (1638–1715), until the era of Napoleon at the turn of the nineteenth century, and this pre-eminence was slow to wane. A century later, at the close of the First World War, the Treaty of Versailles was issued in both English and French, and even now significant organizations such as the International Committee of the Red Cross have a preference for French. Geneva, the city which has the highest concentration in the world of UN and other international bodies, is in the Francophone area of Switzerland. More practically, French has long been regarded as a more lucid, less 'woolly' language than English, and so better suited to diplomatic precision and the niceties of negotiation. Any attempt to replace French as one of the two major languages of diplomacy, for example with Spanish, would certainly be resisted to *la dernière fosse*, as they wouldn't say.

STRAFE

≈ (1915) ≈

ALONGSIDE THE MANY GERMAN terms which have entered English directly over the last two hundred years or so, and which have what one might call a respectable pedigree, there are inevitably a few further words connected with warfare or the Nazi era. **Strafe** deriving from *strafen*, meaning 'to punish', was widely used during the First World War in the slogan *Gott strafe England!* ('God punish England!'), and rapidly adopted by the British as a noun and verb for aerial bombing or gun-firing. An equally familiar expression in the English-speaking world after the invasion of Poland in September 1939 was *blitz* (short for *blitzkrieg* and literally a lightning-war), denoting a sudden overwhelming attack, particularly from the air. Among the German personnel of the Second

World War were stormtroopers (*Sturmtruppen*), as well as *Gestapo* (acronym of *Geheime Staats-Polizei* or secret state-police) and *SS* (*Schutzstaffel* or 'defence squad'). These last two, and especially Gestapo, were and are regularly used as off-the-shelf terms of abuse in English. It is widely believed that Churchill's unwise invocation of the Gestapo in 1945 to describe the prospect of a possible Labour government – because socialism, even under the mild-mannered Clement Attlee, could only be introduced by means of such coercive forces though 'no doubt very humanely directed in the first instance' – was a factor in his loss of power in the election of July of that year. People were offended at such blatant fear-mongering from the man whose inspired oratory had helped them through the war.

The bogey-man potential of the Gestapo, SS, etc. is as nothing to the still very widespread use of 'Nazi' to describe anything vaguely connected to government or any other authority with which the speaker or writer disagrees. A shortened form of Hitler's creation the *Nationalsozialistische Deutsche Arbeiterpartei* (National Socialist German Workers' Party), the term, initially used by the German opponents of the Nazis, was current in English from the early 1930s. Yet more common than the invocation of Nazi is the almost-universal use of Hitler as a standard of absolute evil. There's even a rule created by Mike Godwin, a US lawyer and editor, and known as Godwin's Law: 'As an online discussion grows longer, the probability of a comparison involving Nazis or Hitler approaches one.' In other words, the Nazi/Hitler comparison will almost certainly be made. This casual use of Hitler is sometimes referred to as *Reductio ad Hitlerum* – pseudo-Latin along the lines of *reductio ad absurdum*.

A linguistic casualty of the 1930s to '40s was the word 'Aryan'. Before the advent of the Nazis, this was a fairly neutral term with linguistic and ethnographic associations, one first found in English in the early Victorian period. From a Sanskrit source (*arya*: 'noble, of good family'), Aryan characterizes a major language 'tree' sometimes referred to as Indo-European, including the Germanic branches, of which one is English. In nineteenth-century theorizing, this proto-language was linked to a notional Aryan race which originally populated northern Europe, and then under the Nazis Aryanism was corrupted into an ideology to distinguish white Caucasians from all other racial groups, and specifically from Jews. (Hitler: 'The exact opposite of the Aryan is the Jew.') Nazi attempts to exalt the word have contaminated 'Aryan', except in specialist linguistic contexts. Not by chance, one of the largest gang groups in the US prison system consists of white supremacists known as the Aryan Brotherhood.

BIMBO

≈ (1919) ≈

BIMBO IS THE ITALIAN for a little child (a male one, *bimba* for a girl). A piece of US slang, it was restricted to males for a few years after its first appearance in 1919 before becoming a disparaging term for a woman, sometimes a prostitute. The word resurfaced during the 1980s and, without quite losing the association with prostitution, it essentially combined sexiness with dimness. The minders for up-and-coming US politicians of a certain bent, like Bill Clinton at the start of his first presidential campaign in 1992, were said to be always on the alert for a 'smoking bimbo' (a sign of trouble on the lines of a 'smoking gun') which might foreshadow a 'bimbo eruption', the arrival on the scene of a young woman, maybe several young women, willing to tell all after a fling with the candidate. At around the same time in the early 1990s, the Conservative Party in Britain was sideswiped by a clutch of bimbo-related and other sexual scandals which ironically coincided with Prime Minister John Major's moralizing 'back to basics' campaign (reinterpreted by some parliamentary wits as 'back to my place'). Then, almost as quickly as she had risen, the **bimbo** disappeared again beneath waves like Botticelli's Venus in reverse. But the word spawned a few others: the derogatory 'bimbette', for an even more air-headed and probably younger version of the original, and 'bimboy' or 'himbo' for the male of the species.

ROBOT

≈ (1920) ≈

S TRICTLY SPEAKING, THE FIRST appearance of the word **robot** in English occurs around eighty years before the date given above. In an application which dictionaries term 'historical' (i.e. obsolete), it described an east European system of serfdom in which a tenant paid rent with labour or service. Ultimately, the term derives from an old Slavic term for 'slave'. The modern sense of **robot** to describe an artificial being designed to perform some task(s) comes from *R.U.R.*, a play by the Czech writer Karel Čapek. First performed in 1921, *R.U.R.* (in translation *Rossum's Universal Robots*) is set in a factory that produces artificial human beings for commercial purposes. One of their slogans reads: 'The Cheapest Workforce You Can Get: Rossum's Robots.' Eventually, and inevitably, the robots rebel against their human makers. Karel Čapek was originally going to call his artificial beings 'Labori' but his brother Josef, a painter, suggested 'Roboti' instead.

Words already existed in English with a similar sense to the Čapek brothers' innovation. The 'android' and the 'automaton' enjoyed a vogue during the eighteenth and nineteenth centuries, both words deriving from ancient Greek and describing artificial figures powered by clockwork which could play music and even, in the case of the 'Mechanical Turk', chess. That this last automaton was widely suspected to be a hoax, since there must surely be a living person inside the apparatus (there was), did not diminish the fascination of the curious and slightly unnerving world of androids and automata. But it took the appearance of the **robot** to turn that fascination into alarm since, instead of performing party pieces, it might usurp some real human function.

Within a few years of the creation of the word, there was speculation about what the **robot** could do for human beings and, for the more apprehensive, what it might do *to* human beings. In the early 1940s the science-fiction writer Isaac Asimov used a short story to promulgate his laws* for 'good' robots because he wanted readers to see

---

* Asimov's First Law is: A robot may not injure a human being, or, through inaction, allow a human being to come to harm. The Second: A robot must obey orders given to it by human beings, except where such orders would conflict with

the potential in new technology rather than being afraid of it. But most people continue to regard the **robot** with ambivalence, and the adjectives 'robotic' and 'robot-like' are almost always negative. When in 2015 a Labour MP insulted members of the Scottish National Party by calling them robots, the deputy speaker of the House of Commons had to rule on whether this was unparliamentary language. She conceded that the term might be derogatory but went on, 'For the moment, I am concluding for my own peace of mind that the honourable gentleman was thinking of a high-functioning, intelligent robot and therefore, for the moment, I will not call him to order for the use of the word.' And when, in 2016, the US Republican presidential hopeful Marco Rubio repeated the same formulaic sentences four times over during a caucus debate, he was mocked as Robot Rubio, photoshopped to look like Arnie's *Terminator* (the original bad one, not the good one of *Terminator 2*), and lost badly in the following primary. All this suggests that we have not really made our peace with the **robot**.

Asimov's laws are no longer the stuff of fiction. 'Guidelines on Regulating Robotics' was issued in 2014 by the European Union, the result of several years' deliberation

---

the First Law. The Third: A robot must protect its own existence as long as such protection does not conflict with the First or Second Law.

by engineers and lawyers and also philosophers over the ethical aspects of using robots, together with questions of liability and autonomy. If what is called an 'assistive exo-skeleton' is involved in someone's death, then who or what is at fault? If robots are granted autonomy to make decisions, will they also have rights and responsibilities?

DOOLALLY

≈ (1925) ≈

O NE OF THE WAYS in which language is spread is
not via the essentially peaceful paths of migration or trade but down the rougher road of
military invasion, conquest and occupation. The (Old)
English language was the linguistic beneficiary of just such
a process beginning in 1066 after the Battle of Hastings.
But the process works in both directions. Soldiers don't
only take their own words abroad with their kit-bags, they
bring foreign words back with them. Often these terms
remain at the level of service-slang but a few sidle their way
into general usage.

Deolali is a town in the state of Maharashtra in western India. During the years of the British Raj, this hill
town served as a transit camp for soldiers whose period of

service had expired but who had to wait for a ship to take them back home. They might have thought they'd ended up in a 'cushy' spot (cushy comes from Persian and Urdu words signifying something pleasant). But Deolali was not only a boring place to wait, in some cases for months, but also an unhealthy spot. Malarial fever, called *tap* from a Persian word, was rife. Men who became unbalanced as a result of the fever were said to be '**doolally** tap' or just plain **doolally** and the word became a synonym for odd, peculiar, mad.

As well as cushy and **doolally**, other likely army-related expressions brought back from the east include *gooly*, from a Hindustani term for 'ball' or 'bullet' and rarely found except in its plural slang form of goolies or testicles. Then there's the derogatory 'bint', meaning girl or woman (from the Arabic for 'daughter') and *baksheesh* (Persian) with the sense of present or tip/gratuity but also with overtones of the current British slang 'bung'. Out of *baksheesh* arises 'buckshee' (or free), a word in general use and a piece of army slang referring to an item of kit that has been appropriated, i.e. stowed in someone's room and not where it ought to be in the Quartermaster's Stores. From Urdu comes 'khaki', originally 'dusty' and so yellow-brown or drab and describing the colour of field -uniforms and then shorthand for the kit itself. There is even a slangy term for being out of uniform. A *mufti* is an Islamic cleric – and the

Grand Mufti the highest religious official in a state – but the word has an exclusively Western sense to describe someone out of working clothes, though not necessarily a military uniform ('the Rev Marie-Elsa Bragg is once again in mufti – though, she points out, her working hours are spent in clerical garb.' *Daily Telegraph*). The *OED* speculates that this slightly curious sense could arise from the similarity between the costumed appearance of someone playing a mufti on stage and an army officer's off-duty costume of dressing-gown, smoking-cap and slippers. We're obviously in the nineteenth century here.

A final and slightly poignant example of service slang is a word which those Deolali-stranded men in India would often have used: 'Blighty'. Deriving from an Urdu word meaning 'foreign/European', this was the standard and colloquial way of referring to England or Britain, especially during the First World War. 'Take Me Back to Dear Old Blighty' was a popular music-hall song dating from 1916. One of the things that could get you back to dear old Blighty was a wound. Desperate soldiers might shoot themselves through the hand or foot to earn their passage home.* And a line in the quintessential First World War play *Journey's End* (1929) tells us that even an enemy wound, if minor,

---

* One of Wilfred Owen's most bitter poems is entitled 'S.I.W.' [Self-Inflicted Wound]. It gives a new and grim meaning to the phrase 'he died smiling'.

could be welcome. The commanding officer Stanhope is speaking to a newly arrived junior officer: 'Down to the dressing-station – then hospital – then home. [*He smiles.*] You've got a Blighty one, Jimmy.' But the wound is more serious than that. Jimmy dies, as does everyone else.

AGITPROP

⁓ (1925) ⁓

THE RUSSIAN CONTRIBUTION TO English is small compared to that from most other European languages. True, there are such evocative and culture-specific terms as samovar, vodka, borsch, pavlova (from the Russian ballerina of that name), dacha, steppe, sputnik and cosmonaut. Because of the discovery of large, prehistoric bones in Siberia about 500 years ago, we also have the mammoth, and a useful adjectival synonym for vast, giant, supersize, etc. But the largest number of Russian terms in a single category are to do with politics and authority – and repression.

When Mikhail Gorbachev was the leader of the Soviet Union (USSR) in the 1980s and there was a flowering in relations between east and west, two hopeful Russian terms dominated the headlines: *glasnost*, originally with the sense of 'publicity' but coming to mean 'openness in giving out information'; and *perestroika* referring to the 'reconstruction (of an economic/political system)'. But the general tenor of Russian political terminology is more negative, with even the domesticated English term 'bolshy' – describing a tendency to make trouble or object to authority – having its origins in *Bolshevik* (subsequently Communist). And some words are downright sinister. *Gulag* has been familiar since the publication of Alexander Solzhenitsyn's *The Gulag Archipelago* in the 1970s. Made up of the initial letters of the bureaucratic organization that administered the labour/punishment camps in the Soviet era, *gulag* was applied by extension to the camps themselves. Nor is it any accident that the various Soviet acronyms for their secret police and spying agencies were almost as well known in the West as they were in their homeland, from the revolutionary-era Cheka to OGPU to NKVD to KGB and the present-day FSB. It was Ian Fleming in the first James Bond novel *Casino Royale* (1953) who popularized, but did not invent, the acronymic SMERSH – a shortening of *smert' shpionam*, or 'death to spies' – to describe the Russian counter-espionage apparatus.

Agitprop is an abbreviated form of '*Agitpropbyuro*', a Soviet-era bureaucracy which, as its name suggests, employed agitation and propaganda to further the Communist cause. The word still has currency and is applied in the UK to work, particularly drama ('political theatre') and stand-up comedy, which is supposed to have a left-wing bias. The word can be applied retrospectively. The rediscovery in 2015 of a nineteenth-century poem, 'Poetical Essay on the Existing State of Things', was headlined 'Shelley's agitprop poem granted freedom at last' (*Guardian*). Other politically related terms in circulation include *politburo*, the highest policy-making committee in the USSR and sometimes used to knock any bureaucratic set-up, and *apparatchik*, applied to a party worker but also having something of the sense of the more homely English 'jobsworth'. *Tsar/czar*, used historically to refer to the emperor-like rulers of Russia over many centuries, has enjoyed an odd afterlife in the English-speaking West as the title for someone given wide powers by government to solve a problem: drugs tsar, school behaviour tsar, entrepreneurship tsar. The habit started in the US where 'czar' was used from the late nineteenth century as a casual term for a boss or other overlord.

And, of course, looming over almost all other Russian-based terms is the very next entry: Stalinist...

STALINIST

≈ (1930) ≈

JOSEPH STALIN (1879–1953), THE dictator of the Soviet Union, possessed several nicknames and assumed names, beginning with Stalin itself. Born Iosif Dzhugashvíli, he early took the alias Stalin ('[man of] steel'). During the Second World War and among his Western allies, Stalin was referred to as Uncle Joe, both in himself and as the personification of the Soviet state, in the same way that Uncle Sam embodied the US. More respectfully, the Russians referred to him as *Vozhd* ('leader'). **Stalinist** is an eponymous term, i.e. a word or expression deriving from a name and carrying additional senses and connotations beyond the name itself (see also entries for **Bowdlerize** page 250 and **Mae West** page 321, among others). Dictionaries will define **Stalinist** as nothing more than 'a follower of Stalin' (noun) or 'characteristic of Stalin and his policies' (adjective) but the word has additional layers of meaning which are generally understood but sometimes hard to define. Applied to a government, **Stalinist** suggests a system that is dictatorial and ruthless; it could characterize a military display or march-past – think North Korea – which is choreographed and highly disciplined, while, when used about architecture, the word connotes a building which is functional to the point of ugliness.

Such eponymous terms form a small but significant part of the English language, and they are unusual in two ways. Firstly because their source is not to be found in other earlier words and languages, but in the name of an individual. And secondly because the overtones of such words, as with those nuances of **Stalinist** often overlooked in dictionaries, can be quite wide-ranging and even contradictory. Perhaps the word Dickensian, deriving from Charles Dickens, conjures up a cosy image straight out of *A Christmas Carol*, of snow outside, a roaring fire and turkey on the table. But Dickensian could equally evoke the scenes of poverty and deprivation that he introduces into novels like *Bleak House* or *Little Dorrit*. The term Churchillian is generally employed as a compliment, to describe a national leader's grit or oratorical skills or capacity to inspire, but it could as well be used to describe other facets of Winston Churchill's life and personality: his penchant for bricklaying, his talent as a painter, his skill as a writer of history, his considerable capacity for drink, his tendency to those depressive moods which he called the 'black dog'. All this is to say that eponymous terms are open-ended ones. Because they derive from an individual about whom there may be no final or generally agreed view, they can take on meanings which are different to different people. For some people, to be called a Thatcherite (from Margaret Thatcher and her premiership) would be a term of abuse, for others a compliment.

The process by which a name turns eponymous is curiously revealing. The last five UK prime ministers have all had nouns and/or adjectives attached to them – Thatcherite, Majorism, Blairite, Brownian, Cameronian/Cameroon – but only the first and third have any real clout. The first three are in the *Oxford English Dictionary*, even if part of the Majorism definition is to do with John Major's style of speech. There is a range of adjectival suffixes for eponyms (-esque, -ian, -ite) and the choice of which to use is related partly to the sound of the overall word but may also indicate our attitude towards the person who gave rise to the eponym. So, with US Presidents, we find Kennedyesque and Reaganesque (as well as Reaganite) but also Nixonian and Bushite. The -ite ending has a snappier – more aggressive? – sound to it, while the -ian is quite neutral and, to my ears, the -esque has an almost flamboyant quality. Perhaps that's why we rarely hear talk of Thatcheresque speeches or Brownesque economic policies. In this respect, it is interesting to note that there is no adjective deriving from Clement Attlee, who led the post-war Labour government which, by laying the foundations of the welfare state and nationalizing industries such as steel and the railways, was so influential in shaping the social and political course of the next thirty and more years. Is this adjectival absence because of the linguistic difficulty of attaching a suffix, an -an or -esque or -ite, to Attlee's name without an ugly hiccup in the process? Or is it because Attlee's self-effacing nature was such a marked feature of his public persona that it seemed somehow inappropriate, even improper, to turn him into a noun or adjective?

WHODUNNIT

❧ (1930) ❧

THE HEYDAY OF THE classic **whodunnit** was the period between the two World Wars, often called a golden age for traditional detective-story writing. Describing a highly plotted genre of mysteries in which the interest lies more in the puzzle than in character development and in which the reader is implicitly challenged to come up with a solution before the detective hero, the term **whodunnit** seems to have been coined in the US around 1930. A journalist on *Variety* magazine claimed to have popularized the expression when, in search of a headline to cover a mystery film called *Murder of an Aristocrat*, he came up with 'Spatted Whodunnit', spats presumably being what genteel gents wore at the time. Anyway, the snappiness of the word and what some dictionaries would call its illiterate quality (because it ought to read 'who-did-it') point to a journalistic source.

Even before the name was coined, the **whodunnit** was a somewhat unrealistic form but by the 1930s it became, in certain hands, as stylized and artificial as Japanese Kabuki theatre. There were rules, as in the ten commandments created by Ronald Knox for the Detection Club, of which he and Agatha Christie were founding members (samples: 'Not more than one secret room or passage is allowable'; 'No hitherto undiscovered poisons may be used, nor any appliance which will need a long scientific explanation at the end'). The locked-room mystery was a kind of unofficial Everest, to be attempted because it was very difficult to pull off successfully and, simply, because it was there. The doyen of this sub-genre, John Dickson Carr, included a famous chapter titled 'The Locked-Room Lecture' in *The Hollow Man* (1935) in which his detective Dr Fell, modelled on G. K. Chesterton, enumerates the various tricks used by murderers (and locked-room-mystery writers). From the US, Ellery Queen* interrupted his mysteries before the climactic revelation of **whodunnit** with a paragraph announcing

---

* Ellery Queen was both the apparent author and, along with his New York police father Richard, the detective in a string of tales such as *The Dutch Shoe Mystery* and *The Chinese Orange Mystery* to which the description 'fiendishly ingenious' can for once be justly applied. In fact, the books were written by cousins Frederic Dannay and Manfred Lee using the pseudonym of Ellery Queen.

that the readers were now in possession of all the facts that would enable them to solve the mysteries before Ellery. He didn't need to add 'If you're clever enough.'

The word **whodunnit** has created a few spin-offs or variants. The 'whowasdunin' holds back the identity of the victim, so that the challenge becomes to discover not only who might have done it but who, as it were, deserved to be killed. A recent example is Mark Lawson's *The Deaths* (2013), half satire and social commentary, half mystery. In the 'howsitdun' the puzzle lies as much in the method by which death is brought about as in who did it. Lee Child's *The Visitor* (2000) is a good example of this baffling genre. In the 'howcatchem', or inverted detective story, the identity of the murderer or potential murderer is revealed at the beginning while the interest and suspense lies in seeing whether and how he or she will be caught. The long-running US TV series *Columbo* generally stuck to this formula, with the murder shown early on and then the deceptively shambolic detective Colombo (Peter Falk) closing in on a perpetrator already known to viewers. The classic written text is *Malice Aforethought* by Francis Iles (a pseudonym for Anthony Berkeley), which caused a stir when it came out in 1931 and has never been out of print since. It opens: 'It was not until several weeks after he had decided to murder his wife that Dr Bickleigh took any active steps in the matter.'

NYLON

❦ (1938) ❦

NAMING A PRODUCT OR service can be quite tricky. Failed ones tend to be forgotten, though not always before they have been subjected to general ridicule. Take the Edsel. Named after Edsel B. Ford, the only son of founding father Henry, the Ford Motor Company poured millions of dollars into developing the Edsel automobile in the 1950s and were so confident of success that they neglected to carry out any proper market research. Had they done so, it might have emerged that the not dissimilar German word *Esel* means 'donkey'.

As the year 2000 approached, the British brains behind the Post Office decided that the name, in use for over three centuries, was simply too plain for a dazzling new millennium while the logo, which incorporated the crown, was nothing more than a faded relic. Two million pounds' worth of corporate rethinking and rebranding strained to produce a fresh logo which looked like a swirl of paint colours going down a plughole, and a new name in 'Consignia'. This invented word, apparently combining the notions of 'insignia' and 'consign', managed only to irritate where it did not confuse the public. Within little more than a year, Consignia had been ditched in favour of a bright new brand called – the Post Office.

By contrast, the linguistic creation of **nylon** could stand as a text-book example of how to get it right in terms of simplicity and memorability. The name of the material designates a group of synthetic products that are strong, versatile and lightweight, as well as cheap and easy to make. The invention of **nylon** shortly before the outbreak of the Second World War was timely; it would be used in a range of equipment from parachutes to glider tow ropes to hammocks as a substitute for more expensive and scarcer materials like hemp and silk, the US supplies of which had largely come from Japan. When DuPont developed the new fibre in the late 1930s, the company was focusing on the lucrative hosiery market and went in search of a new name for what had been referred to in-house as 'Duparon' – an acronym for 'DuPont pulls a rabbit out [of] nitrogen / nature / nozzle / naphtha' – or more simply as Fiber 66. They wanted a word ending in -on, as in the familiar cotton and rayon. 'Nuron' was suggested, partly because of an implied guarantee if the word was reversed (no-run) but then rejected since stockings made of the material did run. Changing two letters produced 'Nilon', before y was substituted for the i to avoid ambiguity in pronunciation and perhaps the suggestion of 'nil' or 'nothing'. DuPont decided not to trademark the name, so that customers might think of it as a generic pre-existing material. Other synthetic fibres followed from other companies, including dacron, terylene and crimplene, the last of which may have originated from the Crimple Valley near Harrogate where the ICI Laboratory which developed the fabric was based. None of the brand names, however, have quite the sheeny simplicity or lasting quality of **nylon**.

DuPont introduced their synthetic stockings commercially in 1940; the plural 'nylons' in the sense of stockings appears in print in the same year, in a piece of magazine advice on how to clean them (dunk them 'in rich suds of neutral soap'). Within little more than a year, however, DuPont had to shift almost all of its **nylon** production from consumer to military use. When the war ended American newspapers reported on 'nylon riots' as women queued to compete for restricted supplies of hosiery.

QUARK

≈ (1939) ≈

I T'S UNUSUAL TO BE able to date the first appearance
of a word with absolute precision, to claim that no
one could have said or heard or written the term in
advance of such-and-such a date. Unusual too to identify a single individual as being responsible for that word's
existence. But then **quark** is a highly unusual term, both
in its derivation and in what it describes. It's also a term
which could be said to have both a father and a stepfather.
In his final work, the much admired but scarcely read *Finnegans Wake* (published 1939), James Joyce included the
line 'Three quarks for Muster Mark' in a sequence apparently recreating the cries of sea-birds around the departure
of a ship. Joyce's distorted bird-call seems to be a version

of 'quawk',* and cannot have appeared in print anywhere earlier than 1939 since he made up the word. Jump forward a quarter of a century to the mid-1960s and we find the US physicist Murray Gell-Mann postulating the existence of a set of sub-atomic particles to which he gave the name **quark**, with the explanation that he'd originally plumped for 'quork' but changed the spelling by a single letter because he remembered the word from James Joyce's *Finnegans Wake* 'which I had perused from time to time since it appeared in 1939...'

The world of sub-atomic particle physics can seem almost wilfully bizarre except to those on the inside, an even smaller number of people perhaps than the readers of *Finnegans Wake*. And the bizarreness extends to particle

---

* 'Quawk' is one of a group of words – surely among the oldest spoken ones in the language – which are onomatopoeic or formed in imitation of the sound of the thing described. Other examples include 'crash', 'bang', 'whizz', as well as animal sounds such as 'woof', 'miaow' and 'whinny'. Even though dictionary citations for some of these are comparatively late, for example 'whizz' in the middle of the sixteenth century or 'miaow' (as meaw) appearing in a dictionary of 1632, it seems likely that people must have been imitating a rushing noise or a cat's cry for centuries before such sounds were given the dignity of a written form. The idea, which arose in the nineteenth century and which was christened the 'bow-wow theory' by disbelievers, that humans learned to speak in onomatopoeic imitation of animal noises or natural phenomena like thunderstorms or the sea, doesn't stand much examination. There are not enough onomatopoeic words in any language to provide a basis for meaningful communication and the older expressions, which are inevitably those connected to animal noises, tend to be different in different tongues (to English ears a pig goes 'oink, oink' while to Russian ones it is rendered as 'khryoo, khryoo'). Speech had to exist before onomatopoeic word-creation became possible.

nomenclature. The **quark** has been subdivided into six different categories, each possessing different properties. The first four, namely 'bottom', 'top', 'up' and 'down', appear straightforward enough. Yet 'bottom' and 'top' were originally called 'beauty' and 'truth', perhaps in tribute to the lines from John Keats's 200-year-old poem 'Ode on a Grecian Urn': 'Beauty is truth, truth beauty, – that is all/Ye know on earth, and all ye need to know.' (At least the formula symbols of t and b could be kept when truth and beauty were transmuted to a more mundane top and bottom.) As if to underline the peculiar and poetic nature of this particulate sub-world, the last two of the six types of **quark** are known as 'charmed' and 'strange'.

Altogether the naming of sub-atomic particles is a funny business. Some are erudite, like the 'lepton', from an ancient Greek word for 'slight'; the lepton was also a tiny Greek coin, the original 'mite' of the New Testament. Other titles suggest a mixture of humour and desperation: the 'gluon' glues things together while the 'graviton' is not a lumbering superhero but a hypothetical particle thought to propagate the action of gravitational force. The most literary particle remains the **quark**, not only because of the Joycean allusion in Murray Gell-Mann's discovery but also because of those echoes of Keats in truth/beauty. Giving particles odd or random names does of course sidestep problems of who exactly first discovered the things. The story of

Peter Higgs, and how the sub-atomic particle – the Higgs Boson – whose existence he predicted over fifty years ago has been found at CERN (the European Organization for Nuclear Research) near Geneva, is familiar. There's been some discussion of the parentage of this boson, with five living physicists, including Higgs, having a claim to be the first developers of the theory that a particle of this type must exist. But the origin of the term 'boson' is less familiar. It is named for the Indian physicist S. N. Bose (1894–1974), a reminder that not all scientists come from the West.

MAE WEST

∾ (1940) ∾

MAE WEST (1892–1980) WAS a sexpot, filmstar and actress; though 'actor' might be more PC, it doesn't sound quite right somehow. She was a screenwriter and playwright too, and a mistress of the *double entendre*, as in 'Is that a gun in your pocket, or are you just glad to see me?' **Mae West** earned her place not just in dictionaries of quotations, but in dictionaries of English as well when her name was given to an inflatable lifejacket which was first issued to R.A.F. servicemen in the Second World War. As an American magazine put it at the time, the term was understandable since the lifejacket, when inflated, gave the wearer a 'somewhat feminine figure'. The coincidental breasts/Mae Wests rhyme must have helped too.

Other items of clothing associated with the Second World War include the Eisenhower jacket and the siren suit. The former was a style of military jacket popularized, unsurprisingly, by Dwight D. Eisenhower (1890–1969), the supreme commander of the Allied Forces in Europe and later US president. The siren suit was what is now called a 'onesie', a one-piece outfit originally designed for women to wear in air-raid shelters – because the air-raid siren might go off at any time, day or night, and something warm, modest and unrevealing was required – but later worn by both sexes. The most famous wearer was Winston Churchill, who referred to the outfits as his 'rompers'.

MONDEGREEN

A SMALL CATEGORY OF WORDS should not exist, because they have come into being by mistake. They don't derive from another language. Strictly speaking, they don't even make sense. For example, there's a passage in Shakespeare's *The Merchant of Venice* (1600) which goes: 'Bring them, I pray thee, [...] Unto the tranect, to the common ferry which trades to Venice.' It's just as well that the speaker, Portia, provides a translation of 'tranect' since the term is unique. Almost certainly it's a mishearing or misprint for 'traject', an older word meaning both a crossing-point on a river and the ferry used to cross it. (The modern Italian for ferry is *traghetto*.) Why then does 'tranect' appear in those definitive word sources, *Chambers Dictionary* and the *Oxford English Dictionary*?

Because Shakespeare wrote it, or because his printer misread it.

A word and phrase arising from mishearing and misunderstanding is known as a **mondegreen**. The American writer Sylvia Wright coined the expression in a 1954 article for *Harper's Bazaar* to describe how, when a child, she heard the final line of a verse from an old ballad as:

> *Ye Highlands and ye Lowlands,*
> *Oh, where hae ye been?*
> *They hae slain the Earl Amurry,*
> *And Lady Mondegreen.*

What she ought to have heard is 'And laid him on the green' (and it's also the Earl *of* Murray, not Amurry) but the invention of a romantically named noblewoman keeping company with her dead lover is somehow more poignant. It's especially easy to mishear words when they are set to music so that 'Gladly, the Cross-eyed Bear' is a creative rendering of the hymn line 'Gladly, the cross I'd bear', while Jimmie Hendrix sings 'Scuse me while I kiss this guy' in 'Purple Haze'. (He actually sings 'Scuse me while I kiss the sky.')

The **mondegreen** tends to be connected to musical lyrics, while the related 'eggcorn' is more to do with what's written down as a result of mishearing or some other confusion. An eggcorn, originally an acorn, comes about by an accidental or a deliberate, humorous mishearing, and the term was retrieved from nineteenth-century use by linguistics professor Geoffrey Pullum. Examples of eggcorns, with the 'proper' originals in brackets, are: damp squid (damp squib), foul/fowl swoop (fell swoop), to the manor born (to the manner born), preying mantis (praying mantis), free reign (free rein), just desserts (just deserts). The essential feature of an eggcorn is that, though technically wrong, it makes sense of a kind, while the **mondegreen** probably doesn't. People describe a mildly disappointing event as a bit of a damp squid because of some association between wetness and undersea creatures and because a squid is a more familiar thing now than a squib (a sixteenth-century term for a firework). *To the Manor Born* was the punning title of a highly successful 1970s BBC sitcom that relied on birth and a sense of entitlement, ideas that are central to the original sense/spelling of 'to the manner born', an expression which first appeared in Shakespeare's *Hamlet*. Even the mix-up between pudding (desserts) and what you deserve (deserts) has a tenuous justification, in that both come as the conclusion to a main event with which they are thematically related. One's just desserts are comeuppance for misdeeds, while desserts are just nice puddings that round off a meal.

LASER

◈ (1960) ◈

THE WORD **LASER**, FORMED from the initial letters of 'light amplification by the stimulated emission of radiation ', first appeared in 1960 and within a couple of years it was being used without quote marks or any explanation of what the initial letters stood for, and such absences are a sure sign that a word is well on its way to general acceptance. It might be claimed that acronyms like **laser** are not really examples of borrowing in language since they are put together, Lego-style, out of existing words. But, of course, the words which make them up have come from that wide variety of sources that characterize the creation of English terms.

The linguistic practice of referring to people, processes and things by an abbreviation or a pronounceable set of initials – generally called acronyms – really took off in the twentieth century, but it has existed for hundreds, even thousands of years. SPQR, standing for *Senatus Populusque Romanus* (the Senate and People of Rome), was in effect the logo of ancient Rome while AD (*anno domini*) has long been used in historical dating or RIP (*Requiescat in pace* or 'Rest in peace') on gravestones. Technically these and tens of thousands* of other such abbreviations are known as initialisms because each letter has to be pronounced separately. When the initial letters are run together and pronounced as a single unit, they make up a new word in a sense that neither SPQR, AD or RIP can be called words. Such fresh terms are usually referred to as acronyms to distinguish them from initialisms.

The acronymic habit was given a great boost by the Second World War, and it is no coincidence that the word 'acronym' itself, originating in the US, was first recorded in English in 1940 (it derives from the German *Akronym*). Among the most successful acronyms of WW2, itself an initialism, are radar and jeep, taken respectively from 'radio detection and ranging' and 'General Purpose' (GP),

---

* The online *Oxford Dictionary of Abbreviations* contains over 100,000 entries. Anyone doubting the extraordinary proliferation of abbreviations, acronyms and initialisms in the world should try typing an arbitrary selection of letters into a site such as www.abbreviations.com. A search for ABC throws up a total of 224 entries (which will probably have increased by the time you read this).

a phrase used to describe the unrestricted function of the vehicle. The linguistic point of acronyms becomes clear with 'jeep', which, according to General Eisenhower, was one of the three tools that won the war.* Not only is 'jeep' a single syllable as against the five of 'General Purpose' but it has a snappy, buoyant quality. A less respectable but equally popular acronym from the same era is snafu ('situation normal – all fouled/fucked up') and several variants on it like TARFU (Things Are Really...) or FUBB (...Beyond Belief). More recent acronyms run the gamut from AIDS (acquired immune deficiency syndrome) to the zip/ZIP code used in US postal addresses (and standing for 'zoning improvement plan'). In a few cases the cart seems to have been put before the horse, with the name of an organization or process being deliberately chosen so as to provide a catchy or appropriate acronym. For example, the UK police use the HOLMES (2) IT system in major investigations. It stands for Home Office Large Major Enquiry System. With the rise of textspeak, there is no end to the making of acronyms, initialisms and abbreviations. Soz. LOL.†

---

* The other two were the Dakota, and the Landing Craft.

† When giving evidence to the Leveson Inquiry – remember that? – Rebekah Brooks, the once-and-future chief executive of Rupert Murdoch's UK news organization, caused general amusement when she revealed how Prime Minister David Cameron used to finish his texts to her: 'He would sign them off "DC" in the main. Occasionally, he would sign them off "LOL", lots of love, until I told him it meant laugh out loud and then he didn't sign them like that any more.'

PAPARAZZO

≈ (1961) ≈

ODERN ITALIAN IS A relatively minor but still significant contributor to modern English. As with other European languages like French, German and Spanish, the linguistic contribution made by this particular country and culture may be said to reflect something of its source. **Paparazzo** is the surname of a fictional freelance photographer in the 1960 film *La Dolce Vita*, directed by Federico Fellini. It has been suggested that the screenwriter for *La Dolce Vita* used the name because **paparazzo** is a regional word for a clam, something to represent metaphorically the opening and closing of the camera shutter. An alternative etymology connects the word to a dialect term for the buzzing of a small, irritating insect, something which Fellini himself seemed to confirm in a magazine interview. Whatever the source, the word has become thoroughly embedded not just in English but around the world. The first English use comes in 1961 in *Time* magazine, which defined the subject as 'one of a ravenous wolf pack of freelance photographers', and in a sure sign of the word's acceptability and usefulness it is now regularly reduced to 'pap' or treated as a verb ('You've been papped!').

In keeping with the world of the paparazzi, a number of Italian words and expressions are to do with appearance, display and attitude. It's all about life as it is lived outside, on public view, *al fresco* ('in the fresh air'). This is epitomized by that one-time essential of Italian town life in good weather, the *passeggiata* or 'walk', 'stroll', a leisurely evening amble which gives everyone the opportunity to socialize, to see and be seen. This is tied up with the very Italian concept of *bella figura*, literally 'beautiful figure', an expression whose not very adequate English equivalents are 'cutting a dash', 'looking good/stylish'. *Dolce vita* itself is almost as hard to translate since the literal 'sweet life' doesn't quite capture the layers of hedonism, langour and delight which the term contains. Similarly, *dolce far niente* (literally 'sweet doing nothing' and so 'pleasant idleness') is not a concept very familiar in the English language or perhaps to the English themselves, though Byron did employ the Italian phrase in one of his letters, describing a stay in Hastings.

More familiar in English are *bravura*, meaning 'dash' or 'brilliance' and often applied to some confident artistic performance (first recorded in 1813) and the similar concept of *brio* or 'vigour' (1731). Such qualities might be required by the *maestro* (master), a title of respect from the seventeenth century for a man who has achieved mastery in a particular field, usually music. The term is widely used in the US about eminent conductors. The *maestro* (plural *maestri*) will have to deal with the *prima donna* or 'first lady', the leading singer in an opera company (1782) and so someone of particular significance and therefore, in its usual modern sense, a person (not necessarily female) who is touchy and full of self-importance. An alternative term is *diva* or 'goddess', in the nineteenth century applied to a distinguished singer but from the late twentieth century used pejoratively for a celebrity, often a singer, who is – yes, again – touchy and full of self-importance. An expression which looks and sounds Italian, 'braggadocio' ('loud boasting'), does not exist in that language at all; rather, it derives from the name of a character in a late-sixteenth-century epic poem, *The Faerie Queen*, by Edmund Spenser. He created the word by adding 'brag' to the Italianate ending *-occhio*.

With *prima donnas* and *divas* around, there may well be questions of 'punctilio', a small point of behaviour or ritual and so something which is 'trivial but yet has to observed', used in this sense in English from the seventeenth century. They probably wouldn't understand the word but punctilio, a borrowing from both Italian and Spanish, describes the ludicrous back-stage requirements of rock stars and other slebs: things like Van Halen's demand that all the brown M&Ms be removed from the group's candy bowl* or Beyoncé's insistence that her dressing room be kept at 78 degrees. If these rules aren't followed to the letter the result may be a 'furore', originally used in English for 'rage' in the sense of excitement/enthusiasm but now tending to mean 'rage' as 'uproar'. And if not a furore, then there may follow a 'fiasco', literally 'flask' in Italian, a meaning not carried across into English where it only indicates a failure, usually of a showy, disastrous kind. It also has the same sense in Italian (*fare fiasco* literally, 'make a bottle', 'fail badly') though no one knows why, even if there is a possible theatrical connection. Less severe than a fiasco, though still a mess, is an *imbroglio*, literally

---

* The famous contractual clause excluding brown M&Ms from the band's refreshments wasn't quite as absurd as it seemed. If venues weren't properly prepared because the organizers had failed to take note of all the other band requirements – the more serious ones, involving heavy equipment like lights – then delays, costs and even dangers started to multiply. The presence of the wrong-coloured M&Ms in that bowl meant that the promoter at a Van Halen concert hadn't done his homework. For all that, rock-star/sleb responses to any failure to meet their demands are better described as hissy-fits (a US slang phrase first noted in the 1960s with 'hissy' a diminutive of hysteria), rather than by the more elegant and operatic Italianate furore.

a 'tangle' and so a situation marked by confusion and misunderstanding.

The Italian legacy also includes plenty of food-related terms, which deserve a separate entry (see **pasta**, page 244). But it wouldn't be right to leave the subject without mentioning 'our thing', Cosa Nostra or the Mafia. When capitalized, the latter refers to the criminal society originating in Sicily and its worldwide offshoots and imitators ('the Yakuzas, Japan's tattooed Mafia') or, if spelled in lower case, applicable pejoratively to any sinister and powerful grouping, legal or otherwise ('Fifa is run like a "corrupt mafia", says Diego Maradona' *Daily Telegraph*). The origins of the word, which first appears in English in 1866 as Maffia, described as a 'secret society', are uncertain. It may come from a combination of regional Sicilian words for 'scoundrel' and 'cheat', which derive ultimately from a medieval Arabic term for 'outcast'. A significant figure in a Mafia family is the Don, a title of respect, as with the Spanish Don, the same source as the English university word for a lecturer, tutor, etc. The head of a family is the *capo*, literally 'head' in Italian, a term which was popularized by the Mafia movies of the 1970s and '80s. *The Godfather* highlighted the role of the *consigliere* or adviser to the *capo*, while the films of Martin Scorsese and later the TV series *The Sopranos* introduced to a wider audience slang terms like 'made man', 'wise guy' and 'goodfella', current in the US from the 1960s. It may be better that such things are discussed *sotto voce* (literally 'under the voice') or 'quietly', 'in an aside'. The code of silence which governs Mafia activities is *omertà*, first found in English in 1864 and occasionally used about non-criminal activities ('He demanded a strict omertà of his intimates', from a *Spectator* article about painter Lucian Freud). Without specific Mafia connections, *vendetta*, appearing in English from the middle of the nineteenth century, originally denoted a blood-feud between families (as with the Montagues and Capulets in *Romeo and Juliet*) and then any long-lasting and bitter conflict.

@

～ (1971) ～

@ IS A LIGATURE, A character or piece of type formed out of two letters joined together. Though still found in terms such 'manœuvre' or 'pædiatrics' ligatures are fairly rare in British English while American English ('maneuver' and 'pediatrics') has got rid of them altogether. But the ligature survives elsewhere, as in the linked double-S or *Eszett* in *Straße* on signs for *Strasse* (street) in Germany.

It is possible that @ dates back to the sixth or seventh century as a scribe's way of fusing the two letters of the Latin word *ad*, meaning 'to', 'at', 'towards'. It certainly appears in Europe in commercial lists and records during the sixteenth century. When it first appeared on the typewriter keyboard in the late nineteenth century, @ was known as the 'commercial a/at', and explained as an abbreviation of 'at the rate of', a word/symbol to be used mostly in accounting and invoices. And there, tucked away in a corner of the keyboard, the @ or the 'at sign' would languish for the next eighty years or so, little noticed and not much loved except perhaps by accountants.

In 1971 Ray Tomlinson, an American electrical engineer, was working at a technology company under contract to the Advanced Research Projects Agency of the US Department of Defense on the development of the ARPAnet, the forerunner to the internet. Tomlinson was responsible for the development of a sub-program to send messages between computers. He appropriated the only preposition on the keyboard, the @, and by choosing it for his first e-mail he ushered in a new age of personal connectivity. Tomlinson chose it 'because of its strong locative sense – an individual, identified by a username, is @ this institution/computer/server, and also because...it was already there, on the keyboard, and nobody ever used it.' When Ray Tomlinson died in 2016 he was memorialized as the @ man. @ was 'acquired' in 2010 by MoMA (Museum of Modern Art) in New York which noted that each time it featured the symbol it would specify the typeface used in just the same way that it would indicate the materials a physical object was made from. @, said MoMA, 'might be the only true free – albeit not the only priceless – object in our collection.'

Apart from **@**, there are other quasi-verbal or non-verbal marks or symbols which convey meaning in the place of words. Almost everyone knows about 'emojis' (Japanese for pictographs) like the smiley face image, or 'emoticons' when keyboard characters are employed to represent emotion, as :-) for a smile and :-(for sadness or more specialist examples like >:\ which supposedly indicates scepticism. 'Emoticons' are routine, especially when signing off, and 'emojis' are now standard on many operating systems. But there are ways of communicating by using punctuation marks which long predate the 'emoji' (first recorded 1997) or the 'emoticon' (1988). A short string of dots (...) at the end of a sentence suggests that there's more to be said. 'To be continued...' is the classic ending to an episode in a serial, an ending that is not really an ending. To put a question mark inside brackets (?) is to query the validity of a neighbouring fact or assertion. The exclamation mark, by contrast, is a blunt instrument since it is capable of conveying conflicting responses from shock to alarm to delight, and it may not always be clear which one is meant. Even so, it is a long-established and non-verbal means of communicating emotion, one which dates back to the fifteenth century.

WATERGATE

S OON AFTER MIDNIGHT ON a midsummer's night in
1972 in Washington DC a security guard at the Watergate Complex (a mixture of offices and apartments in
the US capital) noticed duct tape had been placed over several door-latches so that the doors could be opened while
appearing to be securely shut. The police were called and
they arrested five men inside the office of the Democratic
National Committee (DNC), the Washington base of the
Democratic Party. What looked at first like a small-time
if rather peculiar break-in slowly but inexorably grew into
the biggest political scandal of the twentieth century.
For the burglars had not entered the DNC headquarters to
take anything away but instead to plant bugs on the office
phones. And they had connections to the CRP – more

usually referred to as CREEP, the wonderfully apt acronym for the Campaign for the Re-Election of the President. The Republican Party was in power and the president in question was Richard M. Nixon, who was positioning himself for a second term in office; he had a deep, almost paranoid interest in knowing what his Democrat opponents were up to. Not that Nixon sanctioned the burglary, or was even aware of what was nothing more than a low-level piece of criminality. But he became deeply implicated in the attempt, at first successful, to cover up any link between the White House and the activities of the more maverick members of CREEP. Then there was the cover-up of the cover -up...

Richard Nixon was re-elected to the US presidency in November 1972. Almost two years were to pass before his resignation as a result of the original break-in. It was a dramatic but labyrinthine process, with a series of high-level firings and resignations, the indictment and imprisonment of twenty-two of his colleagues, the release of secret tape-recordings* from the Oval Office, Supreme Court hearings,

---

* The White House tapes contained plenty of swearing. When compelled to release them by order of the Supreme Court, President Nixon, who had a buttoned-up and rather priggish image, ordered that various profane expressions should be removed. The resulting gaps in the tape transcripts were replaced by [EXPLETIVE DELETED]. This had two effects: it drew paradoxical attention to the quantity of swearing, just as a row of asterisks will do ('What the f***?'), and it probably made Nixon's swearing out to be much worse than it was, since his apparent preference was for *Christ!* or *hell*. It also made EXPLETIVE DELETED into an ironic catchphrase in English.

threats of impeachment, and the final departure of Nixon by helicopter from the White House lawn. The fall-out from the affair was momentous, politically. It also continues to have a linguistic effect.

Watergate is a Middle English word meaning a water channel or, as two words, describing a gate opening onto water or a place through which water traffic passes, but it is now familiar only as a shorthand term for the US political scandal. So dramatic and far-reaching was **Watergate** that the suffix -gate has been added ever since to any scandal, particularly if it threatens the reputation of a public figure, and use of the term has even spread to non-English-speaking countries like Germany and Greece. *The Oxford Dictionary of American Political Slang* (2004) lists over a hundred -gate expressions and there are plenty more recent ones on Wikipedia. Most are quickly forgotten and some are absurdly contrived, both as names and scandals (look up Donutgate or Flakegate). One of the best, though, occurred in 2012 after a government minister was alleged to have insulted a policeman when he was told to get off his bike and go through the pedestrian gate rather than the main, motor gate when leaving Downing Street. Because of what Andrew Mitchell was alleged to have called the policeman, the resulting furore soon became known as Plebgate. But the coincidence of an actual gate in the affair meant that a few of the quicker-witted columnists jumped on the chance to talk about a 'gate-gate' (see also **fuck**, page 74).

The addition of a suffix such as -gate is a standard way of forming new words in English. Another example is the addition of -lite, a phonetic version of 'light', both to commercial products (carb-lite, Miller Lite) and more generally ('Christmas reminds me how well we do religion-lite in Britain', *Guardian*). Also frequently used is -fest (from German for festival) and tagged on to a variety of words: film-fest, talk-fest, gab-fest, blogfest.

MEME

(1976)

THE EVOLUTIONARY BIOLOGIST AND devout atheist, Richard Dawkins, created the concept and the word **meme** when he was seeking an illustrative parallel to the DNA molecule, 'the replicating entity that prevails on our own planet'. He was looking for another and different kind of replicator, and believed he had found one in the way in which ideas fan out across human culture, 'spreading from brain to brain'. Dawkins explains the choice of name in his book *The Selfish Gene*:

> The new soup [as distinct from the primordial soup in which life arose] is the soup of human culture. We need a name for the new replicator, a noun which conveys the idea of a unit of cultural transmission, or a unit of imitation. 'Mimeme' comes

from a suitable Greek root, but I want a monosyllable that sounds a bit like 'gene'. I hope my classicist friends will forgive me if I abbreviate mimeme to *meme*.

Mimesis is the Greek word for 'imitation'. As examples of the **meme** Richard Dawkins offered: 'tunes, ideas, catchphrases, clothes fashions, ways of making pots or of building arches.' In the years that have followed the publication of *The Selfish Gene* in 1976, the capacity of ideas to hop from head to head has been so enhanced by the internet and its near-instantaneous system of exchange that Dawkins's linguistic coinage is on the verge of becoming standard English. A word search on any news site will throw up hundreds of uses. In an appropriately self-reflexive, duplicating way – look at those two insistent syllables in me-me – the word **meme** has itself become a meme. Although sometimes treated as synonymous with 'mantra' or 'widely held belief', a feature of the true **meme** is that it should undergo subtle modifications as it's transmitted from place to place, person to person. Frequently, however, the word doesn't do much more than characterize fifteen-minutes' worth of online fame: 'Is it a bird? Is it a plane? No, it's a meme. A symbiotic viral meme at that. Once upon a time it would have been called a dance craze, but the Harlem Shake has reached every corner of the internet...' (*The Times*).

Meme, with its intentional echo of 'gene', is not the only internet-related word to evoke some of the attributes of the actual, physical world. From its earliest days, the computer has been likened to the human brain. The entire complex structure of electronic communication, global in extent but invisible, may be referred to as an 'ecosystem', sometimes a 'jungle', having a 'cloud' floating (benignly?) overhead, with its potential to store and then release again the droplets of water (information) that have been sucked up from the ground. There's certainly plenty of water at ground level, for anyone can 'surf' the web, live-'stream' events, or download a 'torrent' file. This is a world that comes equipped with its own underworld, or abyss, in the shape of the 'dark/deep web'. The concept of the 'web' contains an inbuilt ambiguity, depending on where you sit: does it exist to catch things in or is it something to be caught by? The word inevitably suggests the 'spider', which happens to be the term for an automatic search-and-retrieve program, first recorded in this sense in 1993. An alternative term is the 'crawler'.

Difficulties in the system may be local and fairly easy to fix, in which case they can be ascribed to a 'bug', the term which inventor Thomas Edison first used in the late nineteenth century to describe problems with his phonograph (gramophone) because it implied that some imaginary insect had secreted itself inside the machine and was causing trouble. The bug is nothing like as serious as the 'virus', which spreads, infects and mutates unseen; the word goes all the way back to Latin (*virus*: 'venom') and has been in use for over forty years to describe the damage a rogue programme can do online. Almost as old in computing history is the term 'worm' to apply to any self-duplicating program of sabotage. The most notorious example is the Stuxnet Worm, generally believed to have been an American–Israeli cyber weapon intended to slow down Iran's nuclear development. It could be the title of a horror film.

24/7

≈ (1985) ≈

THE DIGITAL ABBREVIATION 24/7 emerged during the 1980s and has now gone global. The first citation in the *OED* is from a US sports magazine in 1983 when a basketball player refers to his jump shot as a '24-7-365', because it's good and consistent all the year through. The first pure dictionary example – that is, 24/7 standing by itself – comes two years later, and 24/7 is now so thoroughly established in British English that it is in the process of driving out older formulas like 'day and night' or 'round the clock'. Its functionality is high. It saves time as well as space. How else could one express the idea of some activity or facility or amenity which is accessible, uninterruptedly, from the first minute of New Year's Day until the last minute of New Year's Eve, without resorting to a long-winded paraphrase like the one in this sentence? An alternative such as 'day and night' suggests a link with nature and the circadian, rhythmic alternation of light and darkness which, if not quite gone, has been largely replaced by perpetual, overlapping work shifts performed under artificial light and in insulated work-spaces. 'Round the clock' doesn't quite work, either. For one thing it takes us back to the days of clock-faces with their fiddly hands and, perhaps, Roman numerals. Also, 'round the clock' may well mean 'shut on Christmas Day'. No, nothing quite suggests the unremitting, never-sleeping, this-is-so-serious-I-can't-waste-any-time-by-using-actual-words world of, well, stuff, as does **24/7**.

This is a very successful digital/verbal American export. So too is 9/11, the instantly recognisable reference to the attacks on New York's Twin Towers on 11 September 2001. Would the date abbreviation have caught on as a piece of worldwide shorthand if America used the British system of dating, putting the day before the month (11/9) rather than the other way about? Possibly not. The long syllable of the 9 rests on the three short syllables of the 11 and is easy to say. It doesn't come off the tongue quite so neatly in reverse. There may even be some buried echo of the convenience-store chain, 7-Eleven, in the formula. By one of those Twin Towers coincidences which send the conspiracy theorists into overdrive, the 9/11 date has the same digits in the same order as the national emergency telephone number (the US's 911 is the equivalent of the UK's 999), which has been in place since the late 1960s. The London terrorist bombings of 7 July 2005 produced the imitative shorthand form of 7/7.

PRECARIAT

≈ (1990) ≈

H ERE'S AN EXAMPLE OF a word which, though coined some time ago, had to wait a while for its day in the sun, even if this is perhaps not the most appropriate metaphor for a term associated with extreme economic and social turbulence round the world. **Precariat** is a portmanteau word, joining precarious and proletariat (for a longer discussion of portmanteau terms, see **Oxbridge**, page 256). Michael Quinion on his *World Wide Words* website says that **precariat** has been 'a term of left-wing writers in English at least since its appearance in the January–March 1990 issue of *Socialist Review*. But it was actually coined in French in the 1980s (as *précariat*).' Describing a sizable social class whose working lives are characterized by part-time or short-term jobs, the requirement to be 'flexible' and available for work at any time, a lack of job security, the absence of any traditional career structure or benefits, and so on, the **precariat** might have remained something of an abstruse political or socio-logical term but for the turmoil which followed the financial crash of 2007/8. The shrinking of traditional employment was already well under way, as suggested by the coining of another portmanteau word 'McJob' (McDonald's + Job) as far back as 1986, to describe the creation of low-paid work in the service sector, but the publication of books and articles on the **precariat** in the wake of 2007 gave the term wider appeal. It achieved some kind of sanc-tification in a BBC survey of 2013 which, after claiming that the old social divisions of upper, middle and working class were out of date in the twenty-first century, came up with seven fresh categories from the elite at the top to the **precariat**, 'the poorest and most deprived class group' at the bottom. Among other new socio-financial terms are the 'sharing economy' for the peer-to-peer exchange of goods and services, and the 'gig economy', the world inhabited by independent workers who take on well-paid but one-off contracts and assignments.

SUDOKU

∾ (2000) ∾

THE **SUDOKU** CRAZE SWEPT the Western world soon after the turn of the new millennium, and the appetite for the 9 × 9 grid became so insatiable that by 2005 one UK newspaper advertised a section in which the puzzle appeared on every single page, while the government-backed *Teacher* magazine recommended it as brain fodder for classrooms. Is it necessary to describe what **sudoku** is? Probably not but, for the record, here goes. The game challenges the player to complete a square partially filled with numbers. The square consists of a 9 × 9 grid which is subdivided into nine 3 × 3 grids; the numbers 1–9 must appear only once in every full-length row and column as well as within each smaller 3 × 3 grid. The difficulty of the game is set largely by the number of squares already supplied with numbers before the player begins, though the disposition of those numbers is also important. *The Times*, in which **sudoku** first appeared in Britain, categorizes its puzzles from 'Easy', in which well over half of the eighty-one squares are already filled in, to 'Super Fiendish', in which less than a third are completed.

The name may be a clue that the puzzle in its current form comes from Japan, where **sudoku** is a shortened version of a phrase meaning 'the numbers are restricted to single status'. But the game itself originated in the US at some point during the 1970s when Dell Puzzle Magazines came up with a challenge which they called Number Place. It was taken up in Japan, a country with a strong taste for puzzling but also one in which the alphabet is not well adapted to that other traditional Western pastime, the crossword puzzle. Wayne Gould, born in New Zealand and a judge in Hong Kong, was responsible for the global fad. Gould developed a computer programme to mass-produce the puzzles, and then sold the idea to *The Times*. The key to its success is its simplicity and accessibility. It's not really a mathematical or arithmetical game at all, though it uses numbers. Rather, since the eighty-one squares in the grid could contain any nine symbols – from letters of the alphabet to tiny images of vegetables or fruit – as long as they are all different, **sudoku** is a test of logic and deduction. The success of **sudoku** popularized other numeric puzzle grids from Japan, such as *kenken* (deriving from *ken*, Japanese for 'cleverness', and meaning in effect 'cleverness squared') and the crossword-style *kakuro* (from running together *kasan kurosu*, the Japanese for 'addition', and the Japanese pronunciation of the English word 'cross').

ANTHROPOCENE

T HE GEOLOGICAL HISTORY OF the earth is divided into differently named stretches of time ranging from many millions of years to the hundreds or tens of thousands of years. In descending order of length these are: aeon, era, period, epoch and stage. Where are we humans now? In the Quaternary or fourth period (so called because it follows on from the tertiary or third period), which covers geological and fossil history dating from more than a million-and-a-half years ago until the present day. That enormous length of Quaternary time is further divided into two epochs: the pleistocene (from two Greek words meaning 'numerous' and 'new/recent', on account of the quantity of fossil remains it contains of still-living species), which lasted until about 10,000 years ago, and the holocene (Greek: 'whole' + 'new/recent') dating from the end of the pleistocene until the present.

The question is whether we are entering a new epoch, a post-holocene one. Plenty of scientists and environmentalists believe that we are, after analysing the increasing impact of human activity on the planet, its spread, its irreversibility and longevity. In 2000, Paul Crutzen, a Dutch atmospheric chemist, and Eugene Stoermer, an American biologist, published a joint article proposing that the new epoch should be called the **anthropocene** not only because of the changes which humanity had already wrought on the earth but because 'mankind will remain a major geological force for many millennia, maybe millions of years to come'. In 2009 a working group was set up to establish two things: whether there should be a formal recognition of the **anthropocene** as a new epoch; and, if so, whether it should be dated from the first use of fire, or from the dawn of agriculture, or the Industrial Revolution, or the beginning of the nuclear age. At the time of writing it seems as though the group will not only agree on the case for an **anthropocene** epoch but also plump for the latest date, a point in the middle of the twentieth century which not only saw nuclear development but the beginnings of significant growth in populations, in carbon emissions, and the widespread discarding of plastics and metals. This human stamp on the planet is far from being a cause for rejoicing. According to academic, walker, climber and ecologist Robert Macfarlane: '"What will survive of us is love", wrote Philip Larkin. Wrong. What will survive of us is plastic – and lead-207, the stable isotope at the end of the uranium-235 decay chain.'

However new the problems, the system for designating different geological periods and epochs as the Quaternary, pleistocene, and so on goes back to the nineteenth century, while the terminology, as so often, derives from ancient Greek. **Anthropocene** is no different, bringing together *anthropos* ('man, human being') and the standard -cene suffix, from *kainos* ('new'). It seems appropriate that the words to describe this fresh and alarming epoch should come from the very language and culture which, in the West, inaugurated scientific investigation and philosophical speculation.

Coda

HUMBLEBRAG

~ (2010) ~

C HOOSING THE FINAL WORD, afterword, postscript,
tailpiece or *coda* (via Italian, from Latin *cauda* or
'tail'), for *May We Borrow Your Language?* was not
easy. The temptation was to go for a word that was very
new like 'phub', a portmanteau combination of phone +
snub used to describe the way a real-life companion may be
snubbed by someone absorbed in their mobile, and admit-
ted to the online *Oxford Dictionaries* early in 2016. But new
words aren't necessarily lasting words, and the 'last in, first
out' principle can operate in language too. Who knows
whether phub will still be around in five years' time?

A word that has already lasted more than five years, that has widespread currency, and that embodies something that is an essential if minor aspect of some human behaviour – or, at least, the behaviour of some humans – is the **humblebrag.** The word was coined by the US comedy writer and producer, Harris Wittels, to denote a Twitter-type statement which boasts about an achievement while wrapping up the boast in a few rags of seeming self-deprecation. Examples of what used to be known as false modesty are legion: 'OMG, can't believe I've just spilled red wine on proof of my latest book!' or 'Totally walked down the wrong escalator at the airport from the flashes of the cameras... Go me.' or what Helen of Troy might have posted: 'So FRUSTRATING when a war breaks out over you... Ugh. Men.' Barack Obama is adept at the more subtle form of the **humblebrag**: 'What the country needs... is an acknowledgment that folks like me can afford to pay a little bit higher rate,' he told Bloomberg News in 2012 when talking about income tax.

Harris Wittels, who died of a drug overdose in 2015, was ingenious in making the word in the first place and, whether consciously or not, he followed a few rules that might be useful to anyone seeking to create a new expression or neologism. To start with, rather than plucking a word from the air, Wittels created a compound term out of pre-existing ones: 'humble' and 'brag' are familiar terms dating back to Middle English. In addition, **humblebrag** has a peculiar and intriguing feature. It operates as an oxymoron (from two Greek words combining notions of sharpness and stupidity), a figure of speech in which a pair of opposing ideas is brought together, as in 'bitter-sweet', 'organized chaos', 'old news'. The choice of the two original words mattered too; the little cluster of 'b' sounds in **humblebrag** help to make it memorable in a way that, say, an equivalent formulation such as 'lowboast' would not be. Finally, and most importantly, there is a need for the word, particularly in the Twitter age. No new expression, however ingenious, curious or glitzy it is, will last unless people actually want it. Like all living language, any neologism has to earn its keep, it has to be useful. Which could serve as an epitaph for the words in this book.